OAKS PARK PENTIMENTO

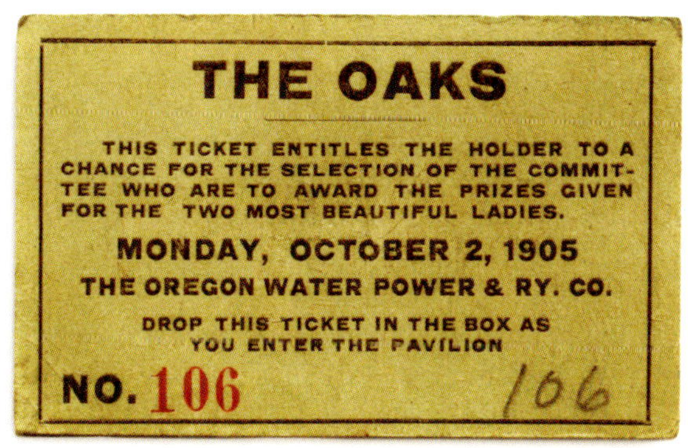
THE OAKS

THIS TICKET ENTITLES THE HOLDER TO A CHANCE FOR THE SELECTION OF THE COMMITTEE WHO ARE TO AWARD THE PRIZES GIVEN FOR THE TWO MOST BEAUTIFUL LADIES.

MONDAY, OCTOBER 2, 1905

THE OREGON WATER POWER & RY. CO.

DROP THIS TICKET IN THE BOX AS YOU ENTER THE PAVILION

NO. 106 106

738 – THE AVENUE LOOKING SOUTH, "THE OAKS", PORTLAND, OREGON.

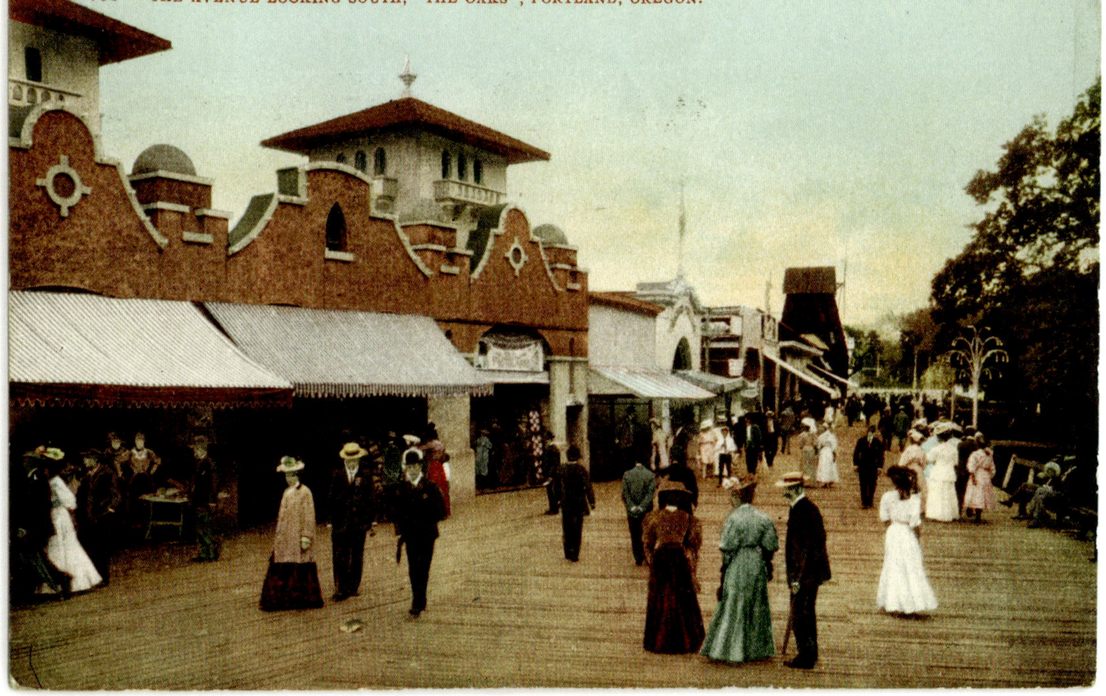

Oaks Park Pentimento

Portland's Lost and Found Carousel Art

PHOTOGRAPHS BY JIM LOMMASSON

INTRODUCTION BY INARA VERZEMNIEKS

AFTERWORD BY PRUDENCE ROBERTS

Oregon State University Press Corvallis

In memory of Terry Toedtemeier

The paper in this book meets the guidelines for permanence and durability of the Committee on Production Guidelines for Book Longevity of the Council on Library Resources and the minimum requirements of the American National Standard for Permanence of Paper for Printed Library Materials Z39.48-1984.

Library of Congress Cataloging-in-Publication Data

Lommasson, Jim.
Oaks Park Pentimento : Portland's lost and found carousel art / photographs by Jim Lommasson ; introduction by Inara Verzemnieks ; afterword by Prudence Roberts.
p. cm.
ISBN 978-0-87071-578-5 (alk. paper)
1. Merry-go-round art–Oregon–Portland–Pictorial works. 2. Oaks Amusement Park (Portland, Or.) I. Title.
NK5033.L66 2009
745.7'230979549–dc22
2009024586

Book design by Steve Connell/Transgraphic Services.
 First published in 2009 by Oregon State University Press
Printed in China

OREGON STATE UNIVERSITY PRESS
121 The Valley Library
Corvallis OR 97331-4501
541-737-3166 • fax 541-737-3170
http://oregonstate.edu/dept/press

TABLE OF CONTENTS

Time, Lost and Found / INARA VERZEMNIEKS 7

Riding Gallery / JIM LOMMASSON 15

The Panels 18

Afterword / PRUDENCE ROBERTS 37

Acknowledgments 40

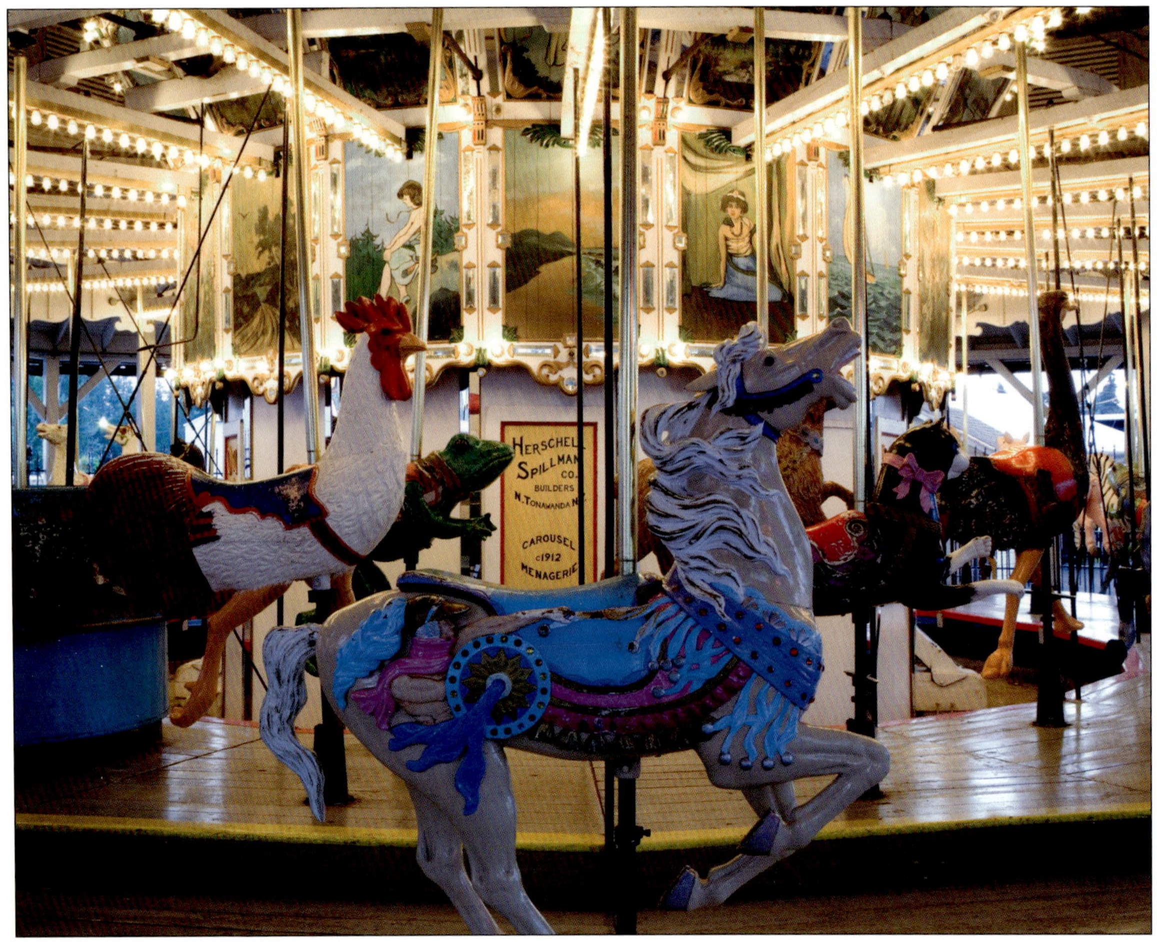
HERSCHEL
SPILLMAN
CO.
BUILDERS
N.TONAWANDA N
CAROUSEL
c1912
MENAGERIE

TIME, LOST AND FOUND

by Inara Verzemnieks

IN 1905, ON AN ISTHMUS along the Willamette River, an amusement park opened—"a combination of reformed Coney Island and a Parisian cafe," the newspaper proclaimed—and inside its grounds, a carousel began to turn.

Coincidentally, the next month of that same year, a young patent clerk in Switzerland published a revolutionary theory about space and time that would have people scratching their heads well into the next century. His work suggested that time is not a steady march from past to present to future—that it is, in fact, much more elastic. Under this new reckoning of time, the past, present and future can actually exist simultaneously.

What could this possibly have to do with an amusement park and its carousel?

Just wait. You'll see.

As one man would discover, this park and this carousel have a funny way of revealing the complexities of time. Here, the past is always present.

JIM LOMMASSON REMEMBERS first being drawn to the carousel as a young photography student in 1970. He had come to Oaks Amusement Park looking for subjects for a class assignment, and ended up at the swirl of skipping horses, dogs, frogs, giraffes, zebras, ostriches, mules, pigs, even a kangaroo.

A different carousel had seen the park through its first eighteen years; in 1923, for reasons now lost to living memory, management installed this replacement, built by the Herschell Spillman Company. Since then, it had taken on the park's unofficial duties as a kind of perpetual wheel of time, going around and around and around, bearing generations of children, parents, grandparents, and young lovers.

The years of service were showing, particularly on the paintings that decorated the carousel's center panels. Paint had flaked and cracked and sloughed away like old skin, revealing a strange double exposure.

There appeared to be two layers of paintings on the panels. The first and older layer seemed to be a collection of idealized Edwardian-era images—a little blond girl clutching a rag doll, a corseted woman pouting beneath a parasol, "exotic" renderings of Arabs and Native Americans. And then, at some point, someone had painted a series of Oregon scenes right over the top of the originals, and pictures of Crown Point, Multnomah Falls, and Mount Hood swallowed up little girls and parasols.

Who knows how long it remained like that, present obscuring past?

But time had other plans. Gradually, air and wind and water raked the top layer of paint away, and the images began to bleed and blur until it was hard to tell where one began and the other ended. Strange and haunting juxtapositions emerged. The little girl reappeared, standing in a pool of water. The road to Crown Point directed you straight to the loins of the parasol woman, who now loomed Amazon-like over the expanse of the Columbia River Gorge. And was that the outline of a sailboat emerging from a thicket of trees?

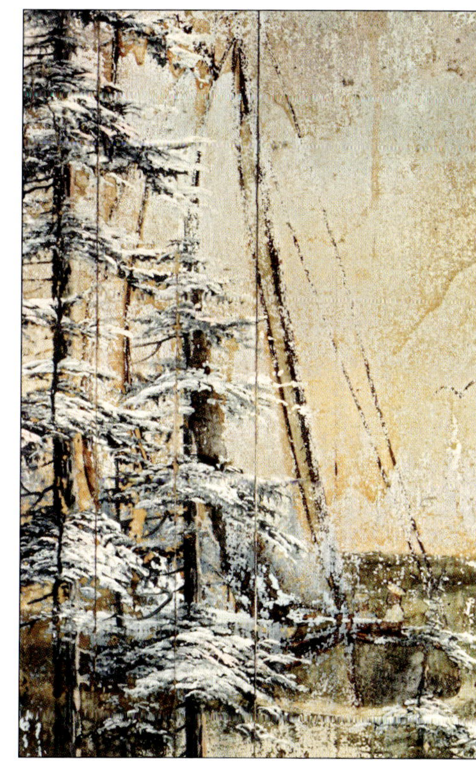

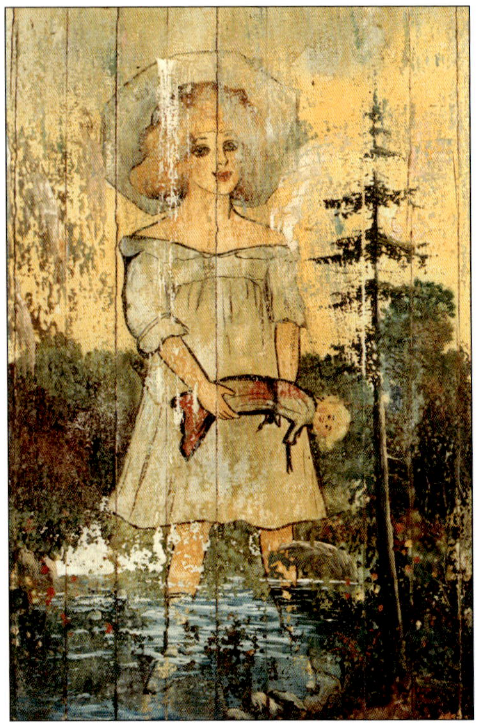

The young photographer was transfixed by these images—they seemed to him "so much more compelling than most of the deliberate work done in the academy"—and he took a few black-and-white photographs that day for his assignment.

Jim had never thought of himself as much of a history buff, but he couldn't stop thinking about those paintings and how he wanted to record their revelations before someone painted over them one day. It took him twelve years, but finally he went back and, with the help of an assistant, over two days he systematically photographed each panel.

Sure enough, just three years later, the park decided to spruce up the carousel. An amateur painting group volunteered to touch up the paintings, restoring the original images as best they could, and the strange double exposures disappeared under a third layer of paint.

Jim, for his part, filed away his negatives of the carousel paintings and moved on to other projects: commercial shoots, a decade-long project documenting boxing gyms around the country.

Then, years later, the Oaks Park images began calling to him again with mystifying intensity. For reasons he couldn't entirely explain, he found himself thinking about them a lot. He couldn't bear the idea that the photographs might become lost or forgotten—"I don't want them to sit in a shoebox, then end up in the dumpster with everything else," he says—and he set about printing the negatives.

It was as if he needed a reassurance only these images could provide—a kind of physical proof of the coexistence of present and past.

FOR MORE THAN A CENTURY NOW, since Einstein published his special theory of relativity, physicists have agreed that time travel is at least theoretically possible. But it seems that traveling forward in time would be much easier than ever going back.

So for now, we fashion our own crude time machines to the past. Sometimes, an object or a place will offer us a way back—a portal, embedded in our contemporary lives, through which we can catch glimpses of long-forgotten history.

Maybe this is why the senior manager of Oaks Park refers to the place sweetly as "a time warp" as she leads you through the grounds toward the turning carousel—past the old dance pavilion, once "filled with pretty girls," according to a 1905 newspaper writer, and "chaps who did their best"—past the midway where crowds once gathered to watch such strange spectacles as "Mlle Mozette's trained dogs" and Prince Karl, "the horse with the human brain and who counts, adds, subtracts, tells the time of day . . . [and] picks out the prettiest girl in the audience"—the "only horse in the world that walks upstairs backwards." (This from a 1906 account in *The Oregonian*, which was immediately followed by the story "Girls Grow Sweet Peas.")

Maybe, from this spot on the river, it's easier to imagine both who we are and what we used to be—ourselves doubling back on ourselves like the carousel's eternal loop.

OAKS PARK, 102 YEARS AGO: From the beginning, this is a place not bound by the limits of conventional thinking. (Note the shift to present tense. This is another way we travel back in time, another way we try to live again in a moment that has already passed.)

Where everyone else sees only a patch of land prone to flooding and littered with shells from the state militia's shooting practice, a man named Fred Morris, head of the Oregon Water Power and Railway Co., looks and sees an electric fantasyland.

Amusement parks, built by trolley companies at the end of their lines to drum up more riders, are going up all around the country. Not ten miles away down river, work is under way on a world's fair—the Lewis and Clark Exposition—which is expected to draw hundreds of thousands of people to town. A competing amusement park could certainly pull in some of that crowd.

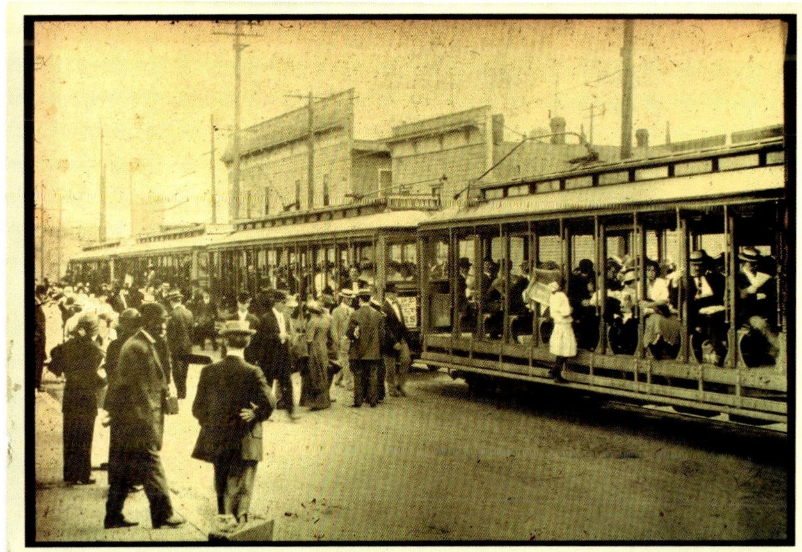

So Mr. Morris throws down a hundred thousand dollars. Because of the pesky flooding, everything is built on pilings. (Park employees will later fish for carp from the back door of the roller-skating rink. Jeanne Pritchard, former president of the carp club, says, "You want to be careful how you spell the word carp," and laughs.)

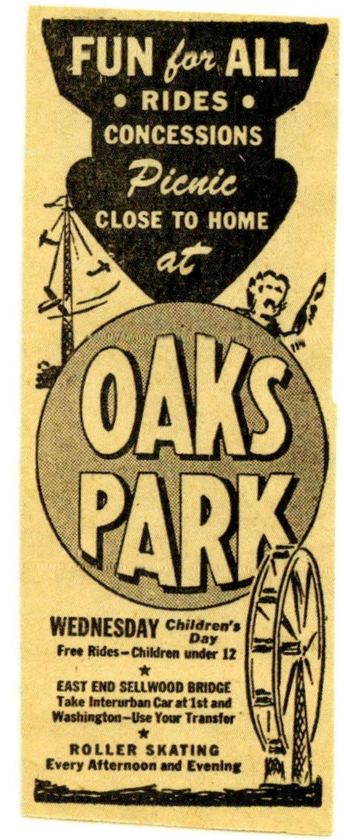

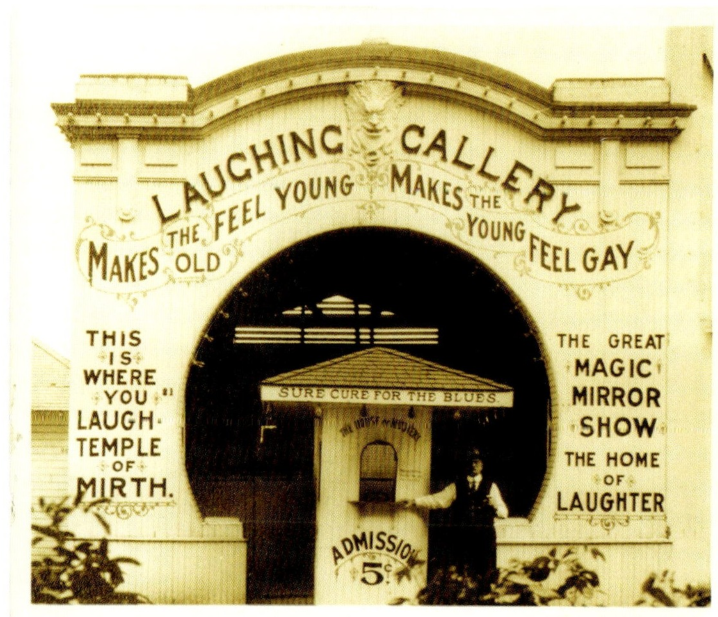

The crowds come strong: Women in massive, broad-brimmed hats dripping with plumage, men in three-piece suits. They hop the trolley for five cents and pay ten cents to get in, their shoes pounding the boardwalk planks past the "Laughing Gallery," past "the chutes" (where carfuls of people shoot down a steep incline into a pool of water), past "Chilcoot Pass" on which people bounce down a bumpy slide on their rear ends—"to the intense amusement of the spectators," according to the newspaper.

There is a building shaped like a windmill, and a Japanese Garden.

Over the years there will also be automobile races, Punch and Judy shows, dogs in pearl-trimmed

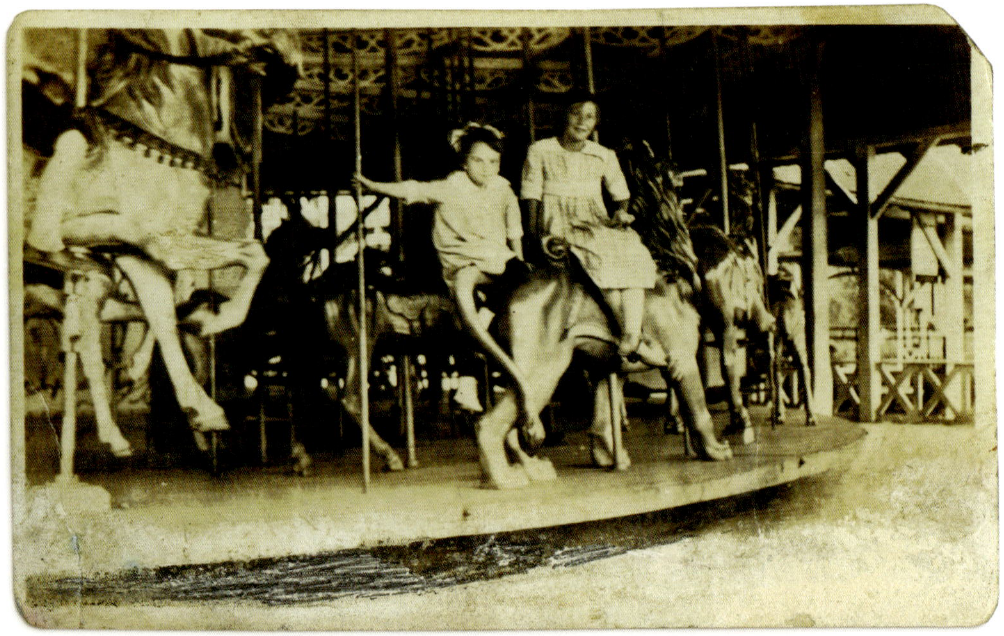

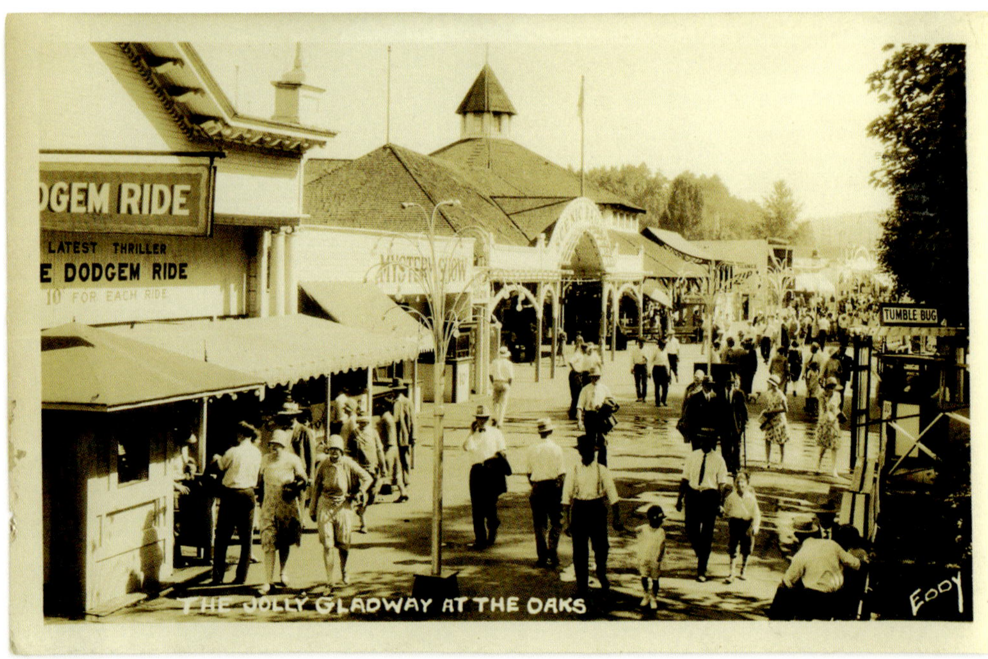

ballet costumes, waltz contests, and daredevil performers sporting ladders and cannons and parachutes, invariably involved in some kind of "ascension." There is an ostrich farm, a monkey house, and a resident bear named Jim who escapes from his enclosure one day and "lustily" paddles across the chutes' pond in an attempt to make a break for freedom, only to be recaptured after about twenty minutes.

There are thousands of electric lights. And beer—for a while, anyway. And dark rides where young couples can disappear together.

It is a strange and beautiful and sexy place. And this makes some people a little scared.

"I have for some time believed the Oaks was a place of danger," the Rev. H.C. Shaffer of the First United Brethren Church thunders from the pulpit one Sunday morning six months after the park opens. The largest share of the blame, he says, "rests upon that class of girls who permit and welcome the attentions of young men with whom they are not acquainted. Every girl of good sense knows when she is in danger, and only a weak, gullible nature would listen and believe all the love trash that a black-hearted wretch whispers in her ear. As for him, he should be hung by his neck until he is dead."

The Rev. H.C. Shaffer probably rejoices when, ten years later, lightning strikes the park three times, blowing up the motor of the first carousel, burning a hole through the skating rink's roof, sending plaster raining down into the auditorium. There are fires and floods—three times, water covers the animals on the carousel. But the park endures. And generations of girls will go on to meet boys who whisper in their ears beneath the dark stands of oak trees.

Today there are no more dancing dogs or escape-artist bears. But a pair of owls sleep in the eaves above the carousel, the park's oldest ride. Women in ostrich-feather hats have been replaced by mothers with tattoos snaking up their arms, carrying babies in slings.

On Tuesday mornings in the summertime, parents and toddlers fill the park to ride the buzzing, blinking child-size motorcycles and spaceships. Then the children gather for milk and cookies while a Dairy Princess sporting a sash and tiara reads a story. When the toddlers leave, bleary and milk-filled, the families and teenagers take over. Two girls take pictures of each other with their cell phones as they ride the carousel.

All their paths trace the same routes earlier visitors followed, though the boardwalk was torn up long ago and the land beneath it filled. Depressions in the asphalt mark where the old pilings are buried.

All this—right beneath the surface.

NOW IS A GOOD TIME to return to Jim's photographs of the old carousel panels, to study them closely.

So much of their beauty lies in what they suggest, the speculation they invite, the way they allow us to see more than what is actually there.

Look at the little girl dressed in white who appears to be standing in a pool of water (Panel 11). This is clearly an accident of time, of flaking paint, and yet it does not feel out of place. Take a closer look at the doll she holds in her hands, the way its body bends, and the hem of its skirt flares to resemble . . . the tail of a fish. What was painted first? Clearly the girl and her doll. But how could the artist so presciently have predicted what was to come, the way the layers painted by strangers, years apart, would intersect, connect?

It happens again and again. Time somehow deposits a frolicking woman, ribbons billowing about her face, into the middle of a field (Panel 3). It leaves another sitting on what appears to be the edge of a cliff—overlooking the Pacific Ocean—as V-shaped birds swoop about her head (Panel 5).

They are beautiful accidents, strange collisions that feel entirely right—a rare opportunity to contemplate all the layers of our history at once.

Because really, we are talking about our history—the history of a city, of each of us, of the anonymous hands that sketch the scenes of our lives. In the case of the carousel paintings, it was likely German and Italian immigrants who created them.

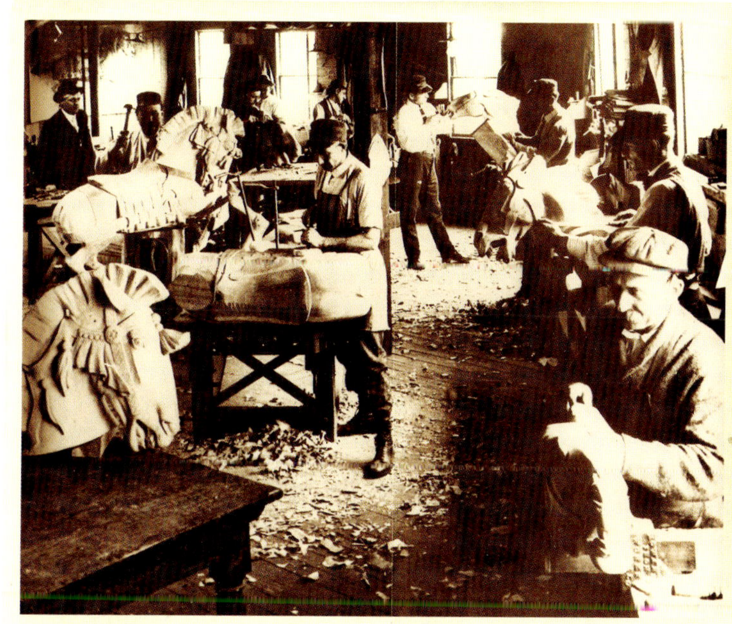

This is the best guess, anyway. As Jim discovered when he started trying to find out who had painted the panels, any complete record of the carousel's original artwork disappeared in the late 1960s, along with the Herschell Spillman Company's archives. Folks at the Herschell Carrousel Factory Museum in North Tonawanda, New York were able to tell him this much: that the original paintings were likely produced in an assembly-line fashion by the immigrant painters, who were forbidden to sign their work to prevent another carousel company from hiring them away. They probably churned out panels for one carousel a week, under the direction of the head of the painting division, a man named Ward Olver, who arrived at work each day with a bottle of gin and a bottle of turpentine. "By the end of the day the bottle of gin would be gone and the turpentine would be half gone," says Kate Mockler, curator of education and exhibits for the factory museum.

As for the second layer—the Oregon scenes—at first, no one from Oaks Park seemed to know who painted those, or when. But then, one day, a man who had done maintenance work at the park during WWII called with a tantalizing clue: He recalled two brothers from Vashon Island being hired to repaint the panels around 1944. He and other workers at the park brought them postcards of Oregon landmarks to work from.

A little more digging revealed that the brothers were probably Wendell Corwin Chase and Waldo Spore Chase, sign-painters by trade who were also known for their woodblock prints and seascapes, as well as their penchant for living out in the woods around Puget Sound, sometimes in a tepee, often without clothes. They both died in 1988, six years after Jim took his photographs, three years after the park brought in a group of watercolor artists called "The Sam Jackson Crafty Art and Buffalo Grass Society" to paint over the brothers' work, now peeling and overlapping with Ward Olver's gin and turpentine assembly-line creations.

"Restoration of Paintings Upsets Purists," read a headline in *The Oregonian* at the time. And while no mention is made of the Chase brothers, or the immigrant painters, or the odd beauty of their combined visions, it is clear that the idea of seeing it all covered up, under a new, more permanent layer of sign-paint, was unsettling to people. Even to a few of the Buffalo Grass Society volunteers. "Some of them expressed a measure of dismay at the necessity of covering up some of the original scenes in favor of embellishing the more prominent figures," according to the article.

But the painting went on, despite this fear of loss. (Because of this fear of loss?)

Meanwhile, Jim's negatives waited.

SOMETIMES THINGS REVEAL THEMSELVES for reasons we don't understand until later—a strange juxtaposition of seemingly random images and events that gradually come into clearer focus.

It might help to know that as Jim Lommasson found himself thinking with increasing intensity about the carousel images he had captured twenty years ago, and their blurring of past and present, he was slowly helping his ninety-one-year-old mother and eighty-four-year-old father move from the North Portland home where they had lived for forty years to an assisted-living facility.

By day he would work on the prints, pulling them together as you would a family album, readying them for an exhibit at the Portland Art Museum that he had decided to call "Oaks Park Pentimento."

In the evening, he would go help his parents pack. One night, after they had left for their new home, he walked through the house and looked at what remained.

There was his mother's birth certificate, the notice of her mother's funeral, postcards that his father had written to his parents from Fort Lewis, Washington. Weeks later, his father would ship off to fight in the Battle of the Bulge. And under the weight of all those memories, he was overcome.

What do we keep? And what do we leave behind?

He tells this story standing in the Oaks Park parking lot, within a few hundred yards of the carousel.

And you want to tell him: Look at your photographs. Watch the carousel, which continues to go around and around and around until the edges of the world overlap and smudge, until you can't tell anymore where things begin and end. Maybe the demarcation is not as clear as we think.

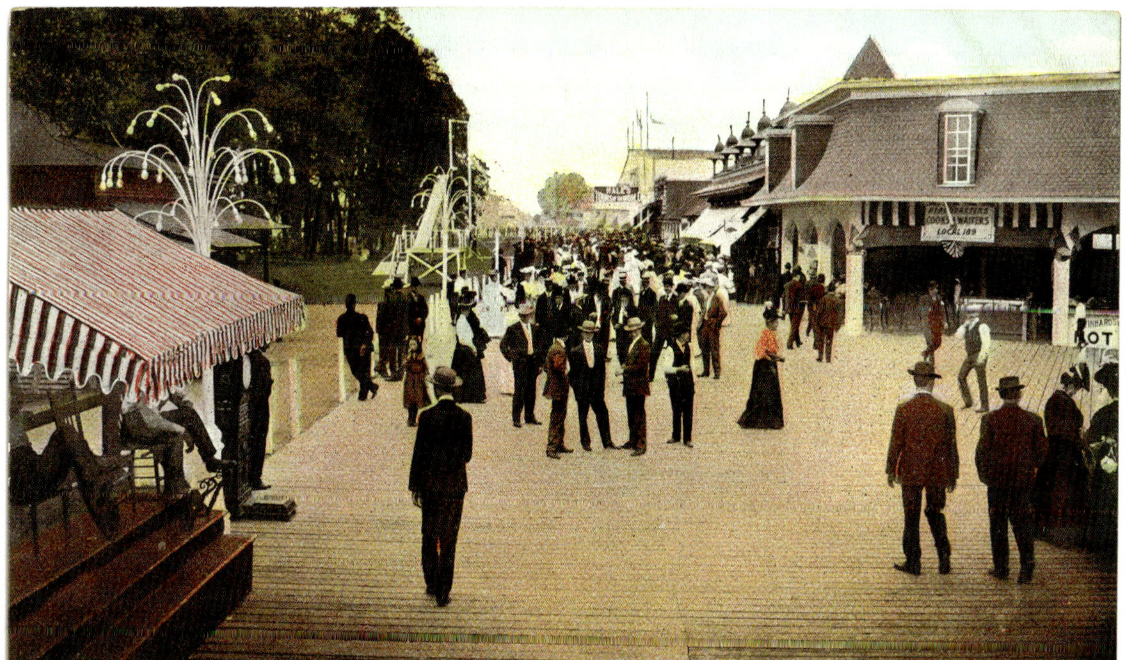

5517. On the Avenue at Oaks, Portland, Ore.

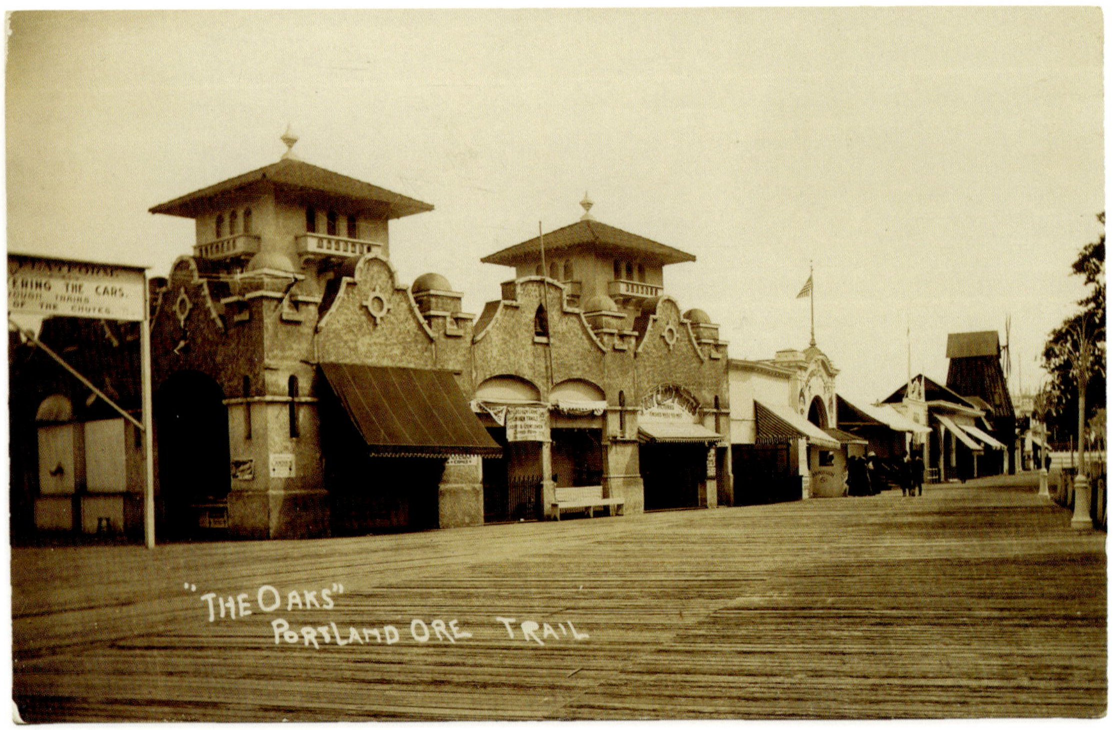
"THE OAKS"
PORTLAND ORE. TRAIL

RIDING GALLERY

by Jim Lommasson

IT WAS LOVE AT . . . second glance.

When I first started going to Oaks Amusement Park in the '60s, it was like many other aging amusement parks across America. They had all seen better days. The Oaks, once called the Coney Island on the Willamette, had been a colorful focal point of social life in Portland, Oregon's Sellwood district—it had all the usual attractions, and more. I especially loved the park in the winter. It was closed, lonely, neglected, and full of ghosts. I loved the boarded up "Laughing Gallery" and the bleak "Fun Games" arcade. I liked to crawl around the buttoned-down rides, walk the spooky, vacant, drizzly midway and climb around the old equipment boneyard with its remnants of rides long forgotten. But I always gravitated to the carousel. It's called a "Noah's Ark" carousel, or a menagerie carousel. All kinds of animals are represented, and there are lots of them. The beautiful hand-carved animals get all the attention.

Carousels, sometimes called riding galleries, date back to the twelfth century. According to folklore, Arab horsemen played a game in which they threw clay balls at each other while riding in a circle. Spanish and Italian soldiers became acquainted with the game during the Crusades. They adopted the game, brought it back to their homelands, and called it "Carosello" (little war). A version of the pastime, called "carrousel," became a favorite of the court in France at the beginning of the seventeenth century. In 1662, Louis XIV entertained his lady friend, Louise de La Vallière, with a gigantic event involving hundreds of knights riding in formation around a Paris square, which to this day is called "Place du Carrousel." Eventually, an imaginative Parisian toy maker duplicated this colorful spectacle, crafting a miniature model of the carousel small enough for children to ride. At some point, decorations—including a gallery of paintings—were added to the center poles of carousels to help prevent dizziness. If the swirl of the spinning world to their right bothered riders, they could look to their left and see soothing imagery that turned at the same speed as the rest of the carousel.*

When I first noticed the paintings in the center column of the Oaks Park carousel, I realized that I had been seeing them, but not *really* seeing them. They were hidden behind a menagerie of dragons, tigers, frogs, giraffes, and horses. It took a while before I paid attention to the strange and beautiful tattered paintings on the center pole of the carousel. The images were bewildering and almost mystical. They didn't make sense. I realized they were special and deserved a second look. The eighteen panels contained an unexplainable, confounding amalgamation of imagery. How did this happen? There was a sophisticated woman emerging like a giant from a dwarfed Crown Point with a trail to a tiny Vista House; an Indian chief looming over the Columbia Gorge; a sailboat floating through a snowy forest; and a dancing hootchie-kootchie girl with Multnomah Falls flowing from her face. In 1970, I photographed the Parasol woman with the Vista House in black and white for a college photography-class assignment. Later, I did some research

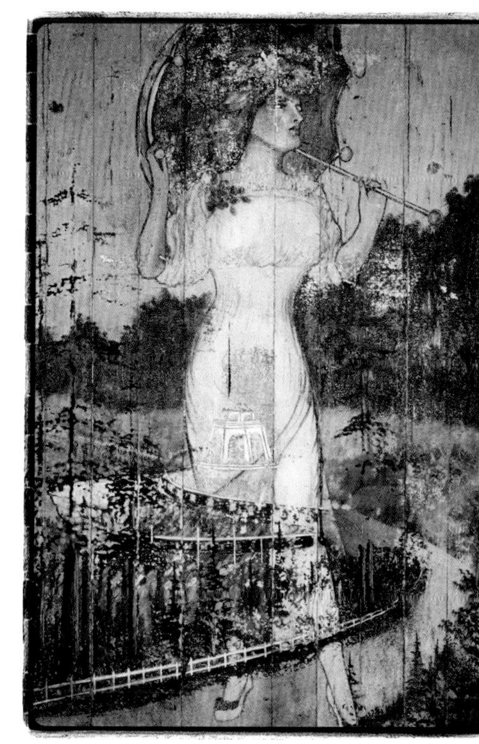

and learned how two layers of paintings merged to form the odd, whimsical images that I'd found so entrancing. The first layer, painted in 1912, showed a series of romanticized renderings of fashionable ladies, explorers, young girls, and pastoral scenes. The visual icons of the imagery became idealized characters constructed out of a kind of voyeurism extended to the exoticism of other races and cultures. The second layer of imagery, painted in 1944, depicted Oregon landmarks: Multnomah Falls, Mount Hood, the Oregon coast, and the Columbia Gorge. After many years and two floods, the latter paintings began to flake off. A series of accidental compositions remained—they were like photographic "double exposures."

As the paint has worn off, the natural excavation of these images—and the cultural values they represent—come back to haunt us. The hovering apparitions claim the ground below them, as our collective consciousness is taunted by their pioneer story. Juxtaposed and suspended in time, they deconstruct themselves. On some of the panels, the ghosts of the past are still hidden, and their absence is felt in the vastness and stillness of the landscape.

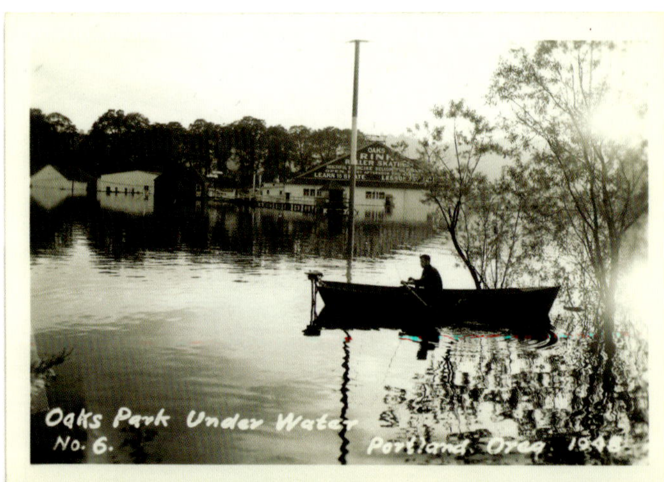

The tattered paintings were a result of the work of two generations of artists long gone, and the forces of nature—wind, rain, floods—and neglect. How many revolutions might the carousel have turned since 1912? And how did a series of floods—including the 1948 Vanport Flood that submerged the carousel—leave their mark? My parents' home was washed away in that flood.

When I examined the paintings more closely, I thought they looked like the ancient frescoes of Pompeii and Herculaneum. There seemed strange evidence of evolution and creation and chaos theory—all at the same time. Or maybe just wear and tear and urban renewal. But they were (our) Pompeii. They were part of Portland's visual and cultural history, and needed to be documented before something happened to them. I photographed the paintings in 1982 with the diligence and precision of an archeologist preserving some ancient ruin before it finally collapses. I was afraid the evidence of these beautiful objects of art and history would simply evaporate from memory. As I had foreseen, in 1985 the panels were overpainted again with a new hybrid version of the imagery, and it appears that my photographs are the only remaining record of the metamorphosed images. So I guess I've done my job: I've added a few pages to Portland's family album.

In 2007, after dusting off the old negatives in preparation for an exhibition of the collection at the Portland Art Museum, I had a dream one night. I dreamed that as I was researching the history of the old carousel, I crawled beneath the pilings of the buildings at Oaks Park to discover the amusement park's boneyard. There, in a dark, dusty pile, among rusting and broken pieces of Ferris wheels, dented bumper cars, and midway signs, were the individual painted boards from the carousel paintings, piled like firewood: the pieces of the paintings I had photographed thirty years ago. In my dream, I was elated—they had not been destroyed, after all! Alas, it was only a wishful dream.

I trust old ghosts, in fifty or a hundred years, will find their way to visit us again.

And I hope someone will take a picture.

*The historical information here is drawn from James Huddleston's article, "The Magic Merry Go Round" (*Pageant*, 1957).

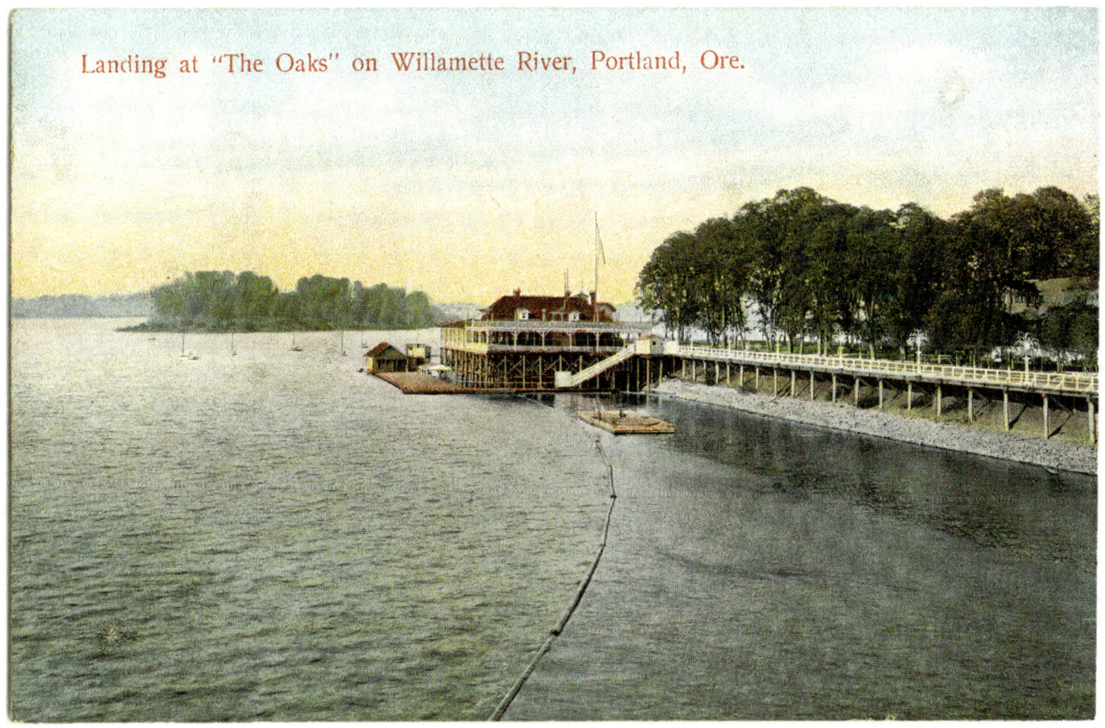
Landing at "The Oaks" on Willamette River, Portland, Ore.

PANEL 1

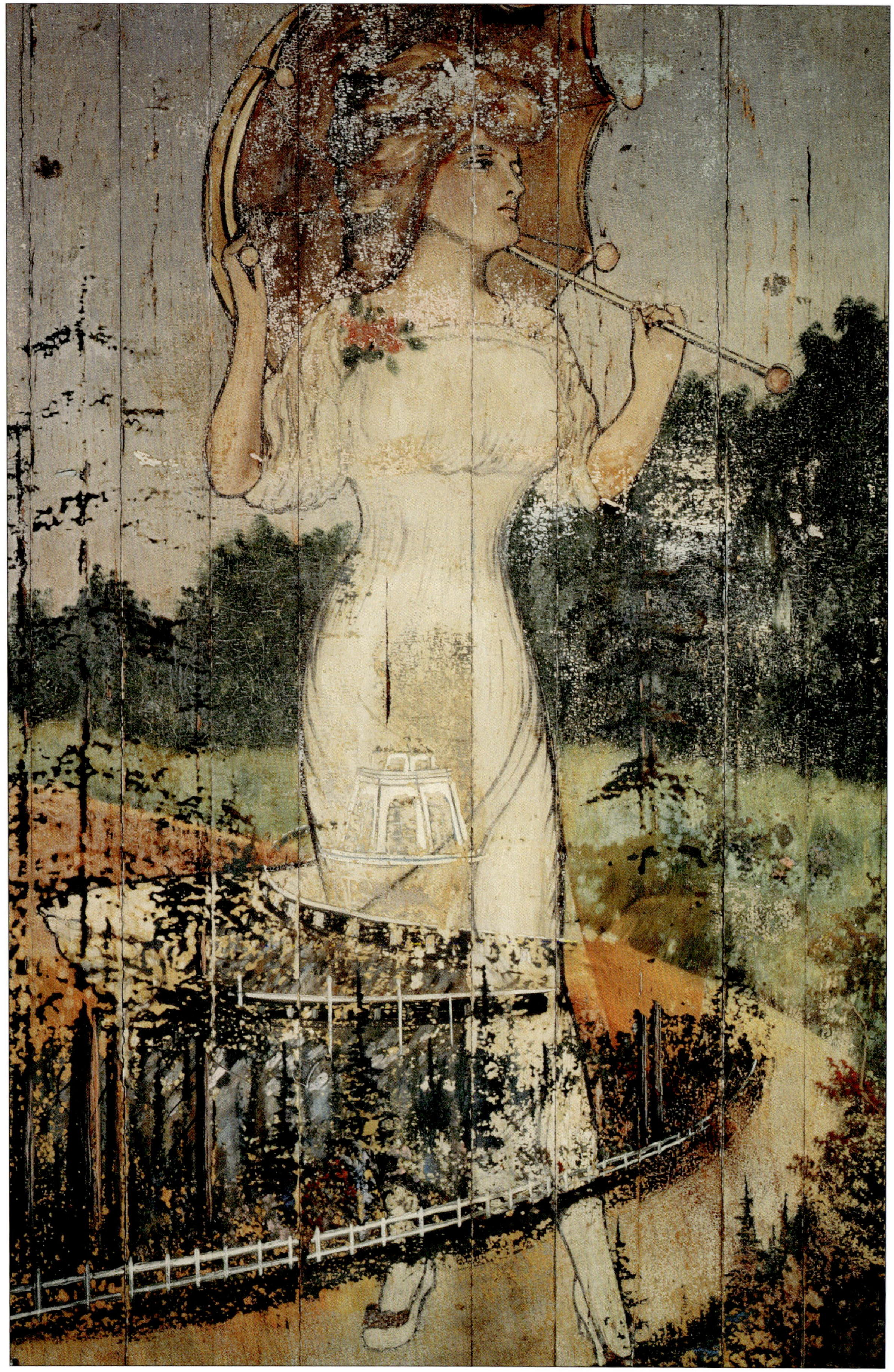

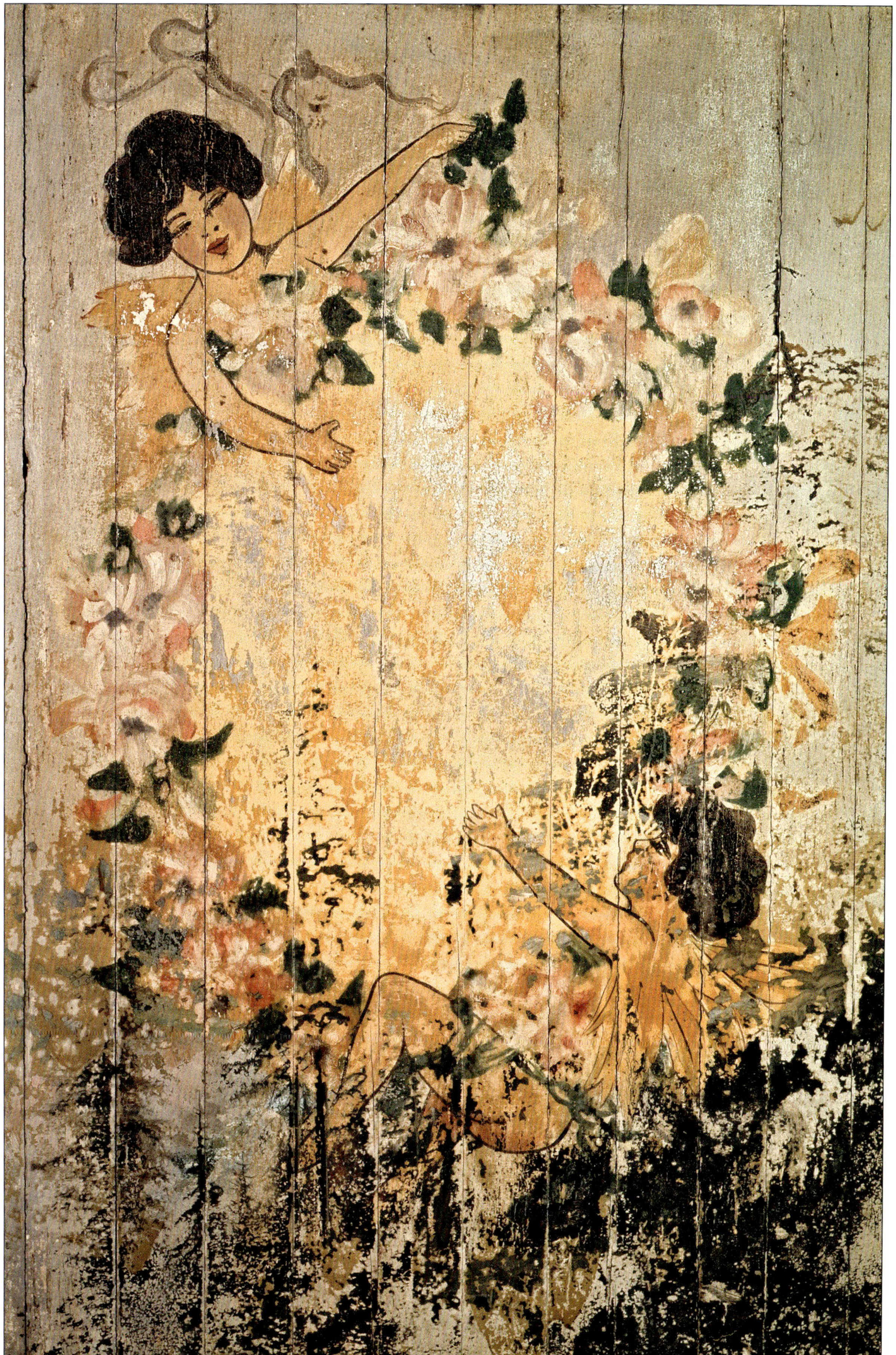

PANEL 2

PANEL 3

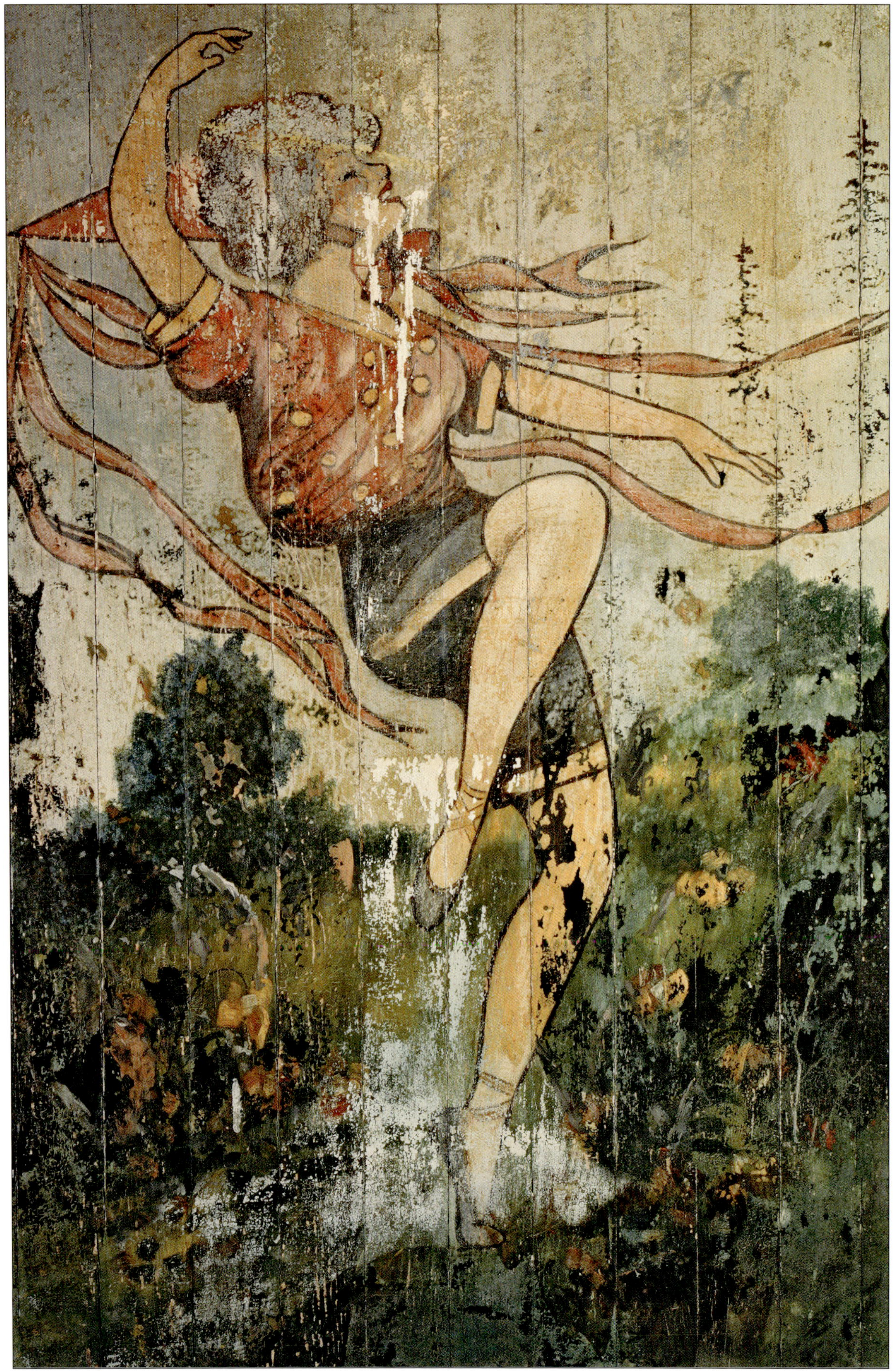

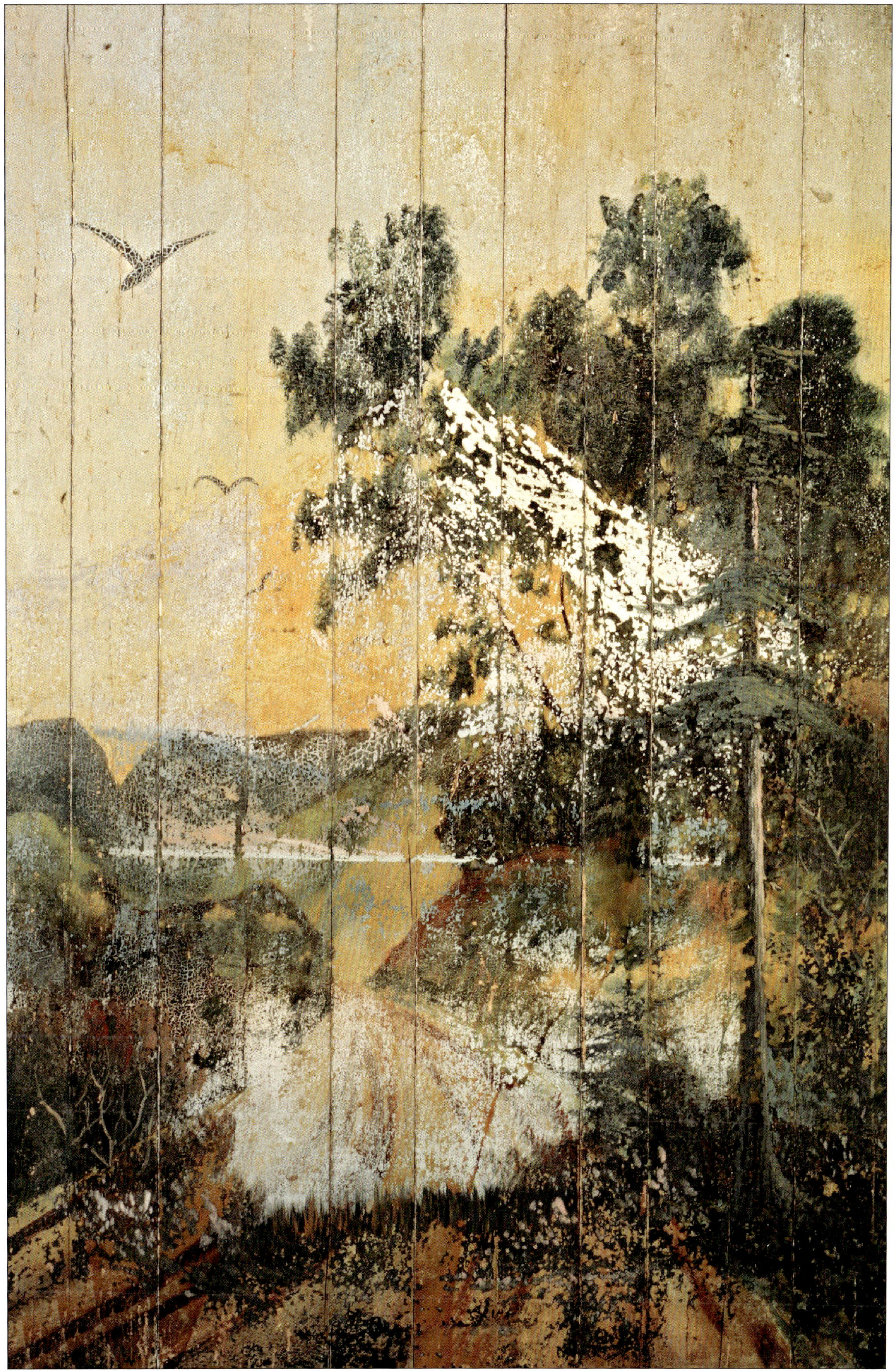

PANEL 4

PANEL 5

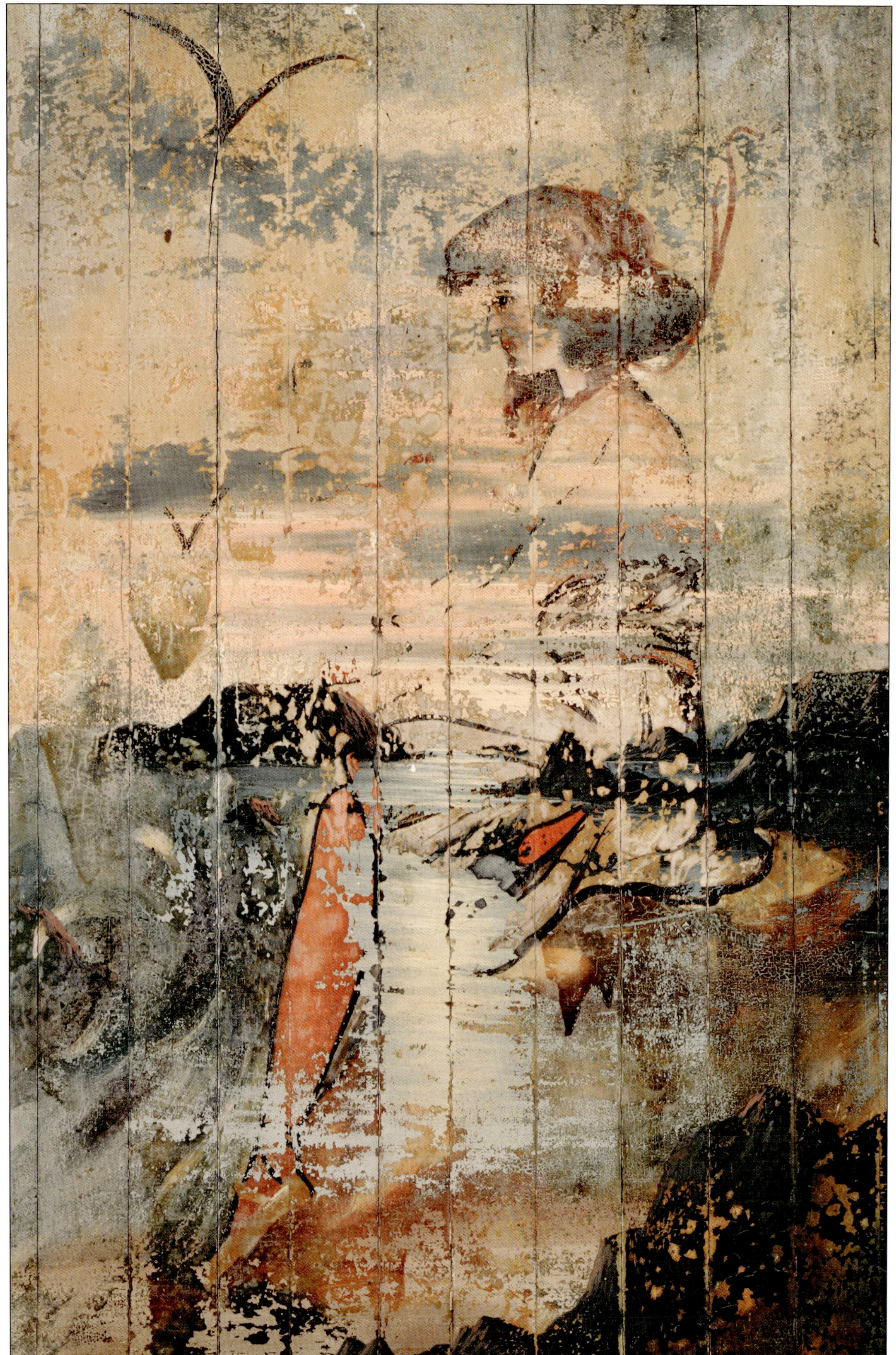

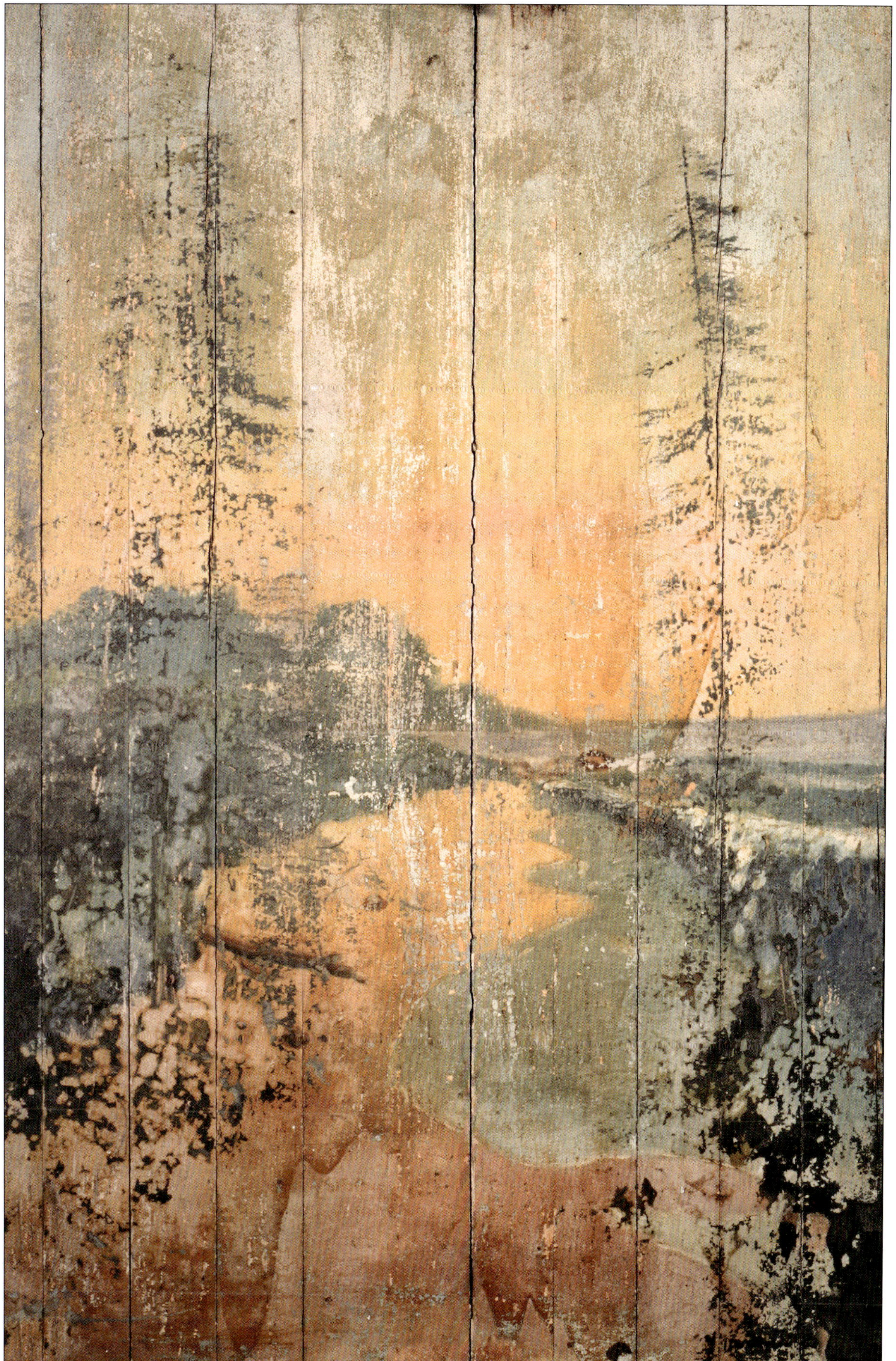

PANEL 6

PANEL 7

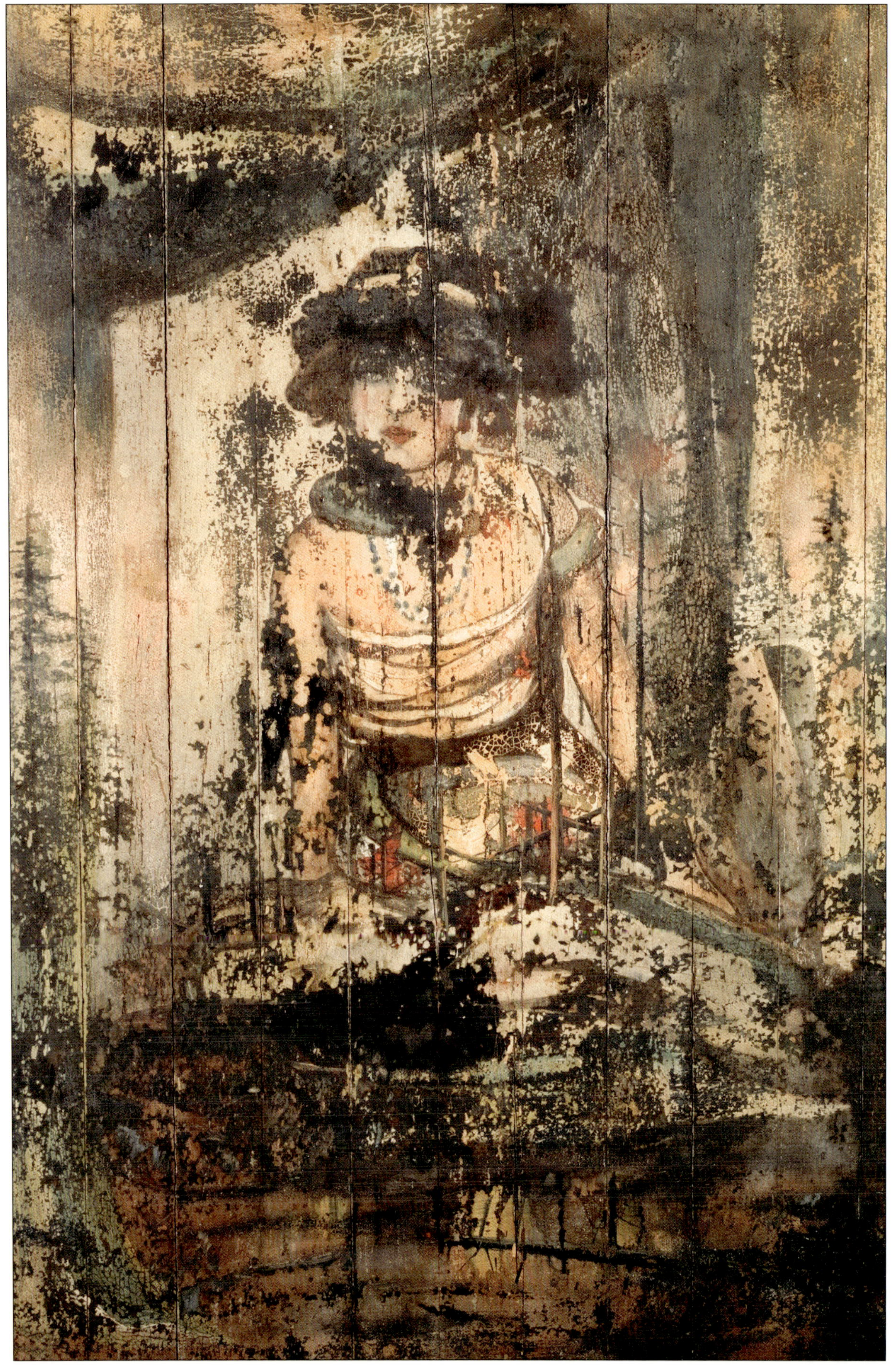

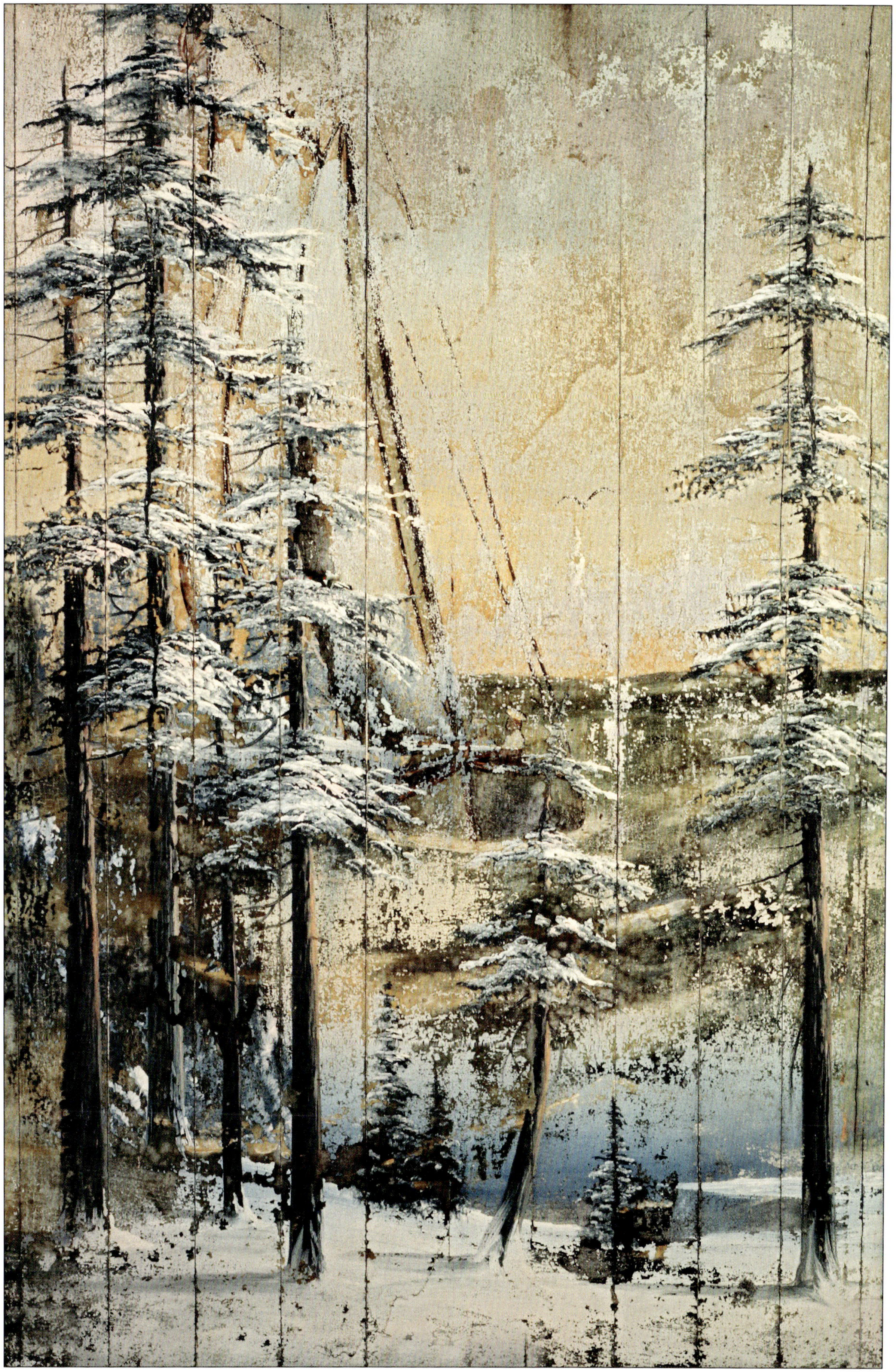

PANEL 8

PANEL 9

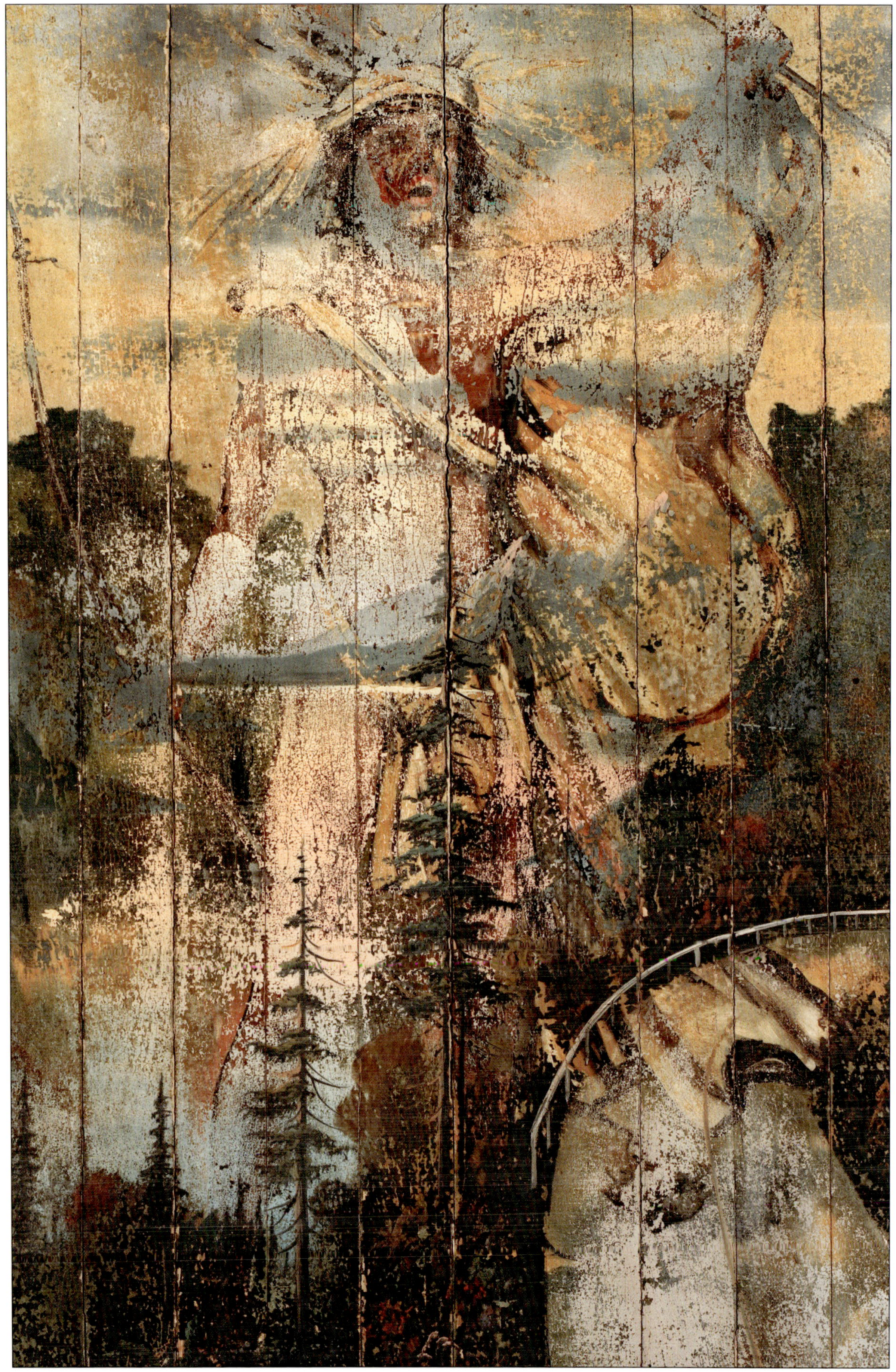

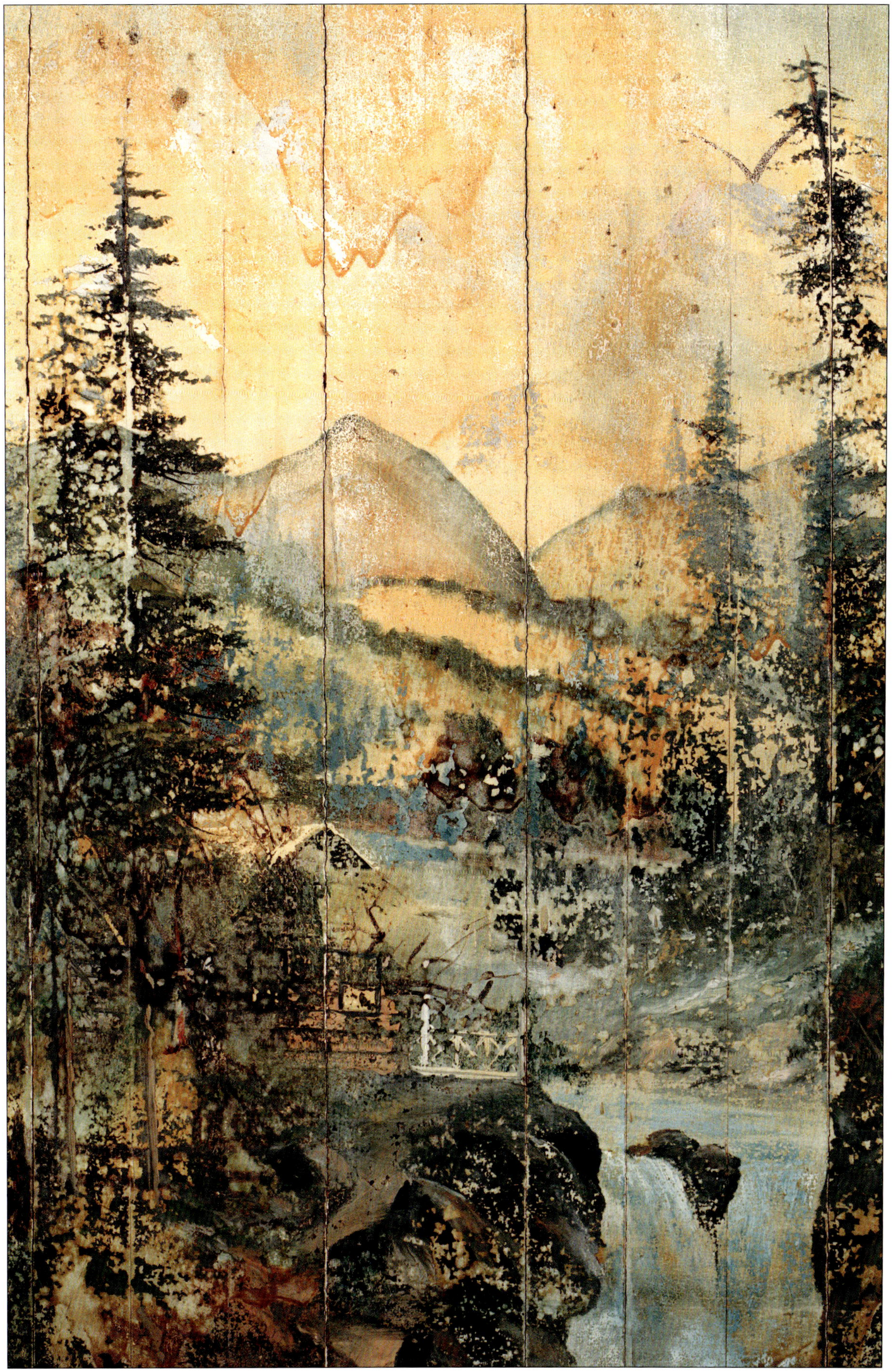

PANEL 10

PANEL 11

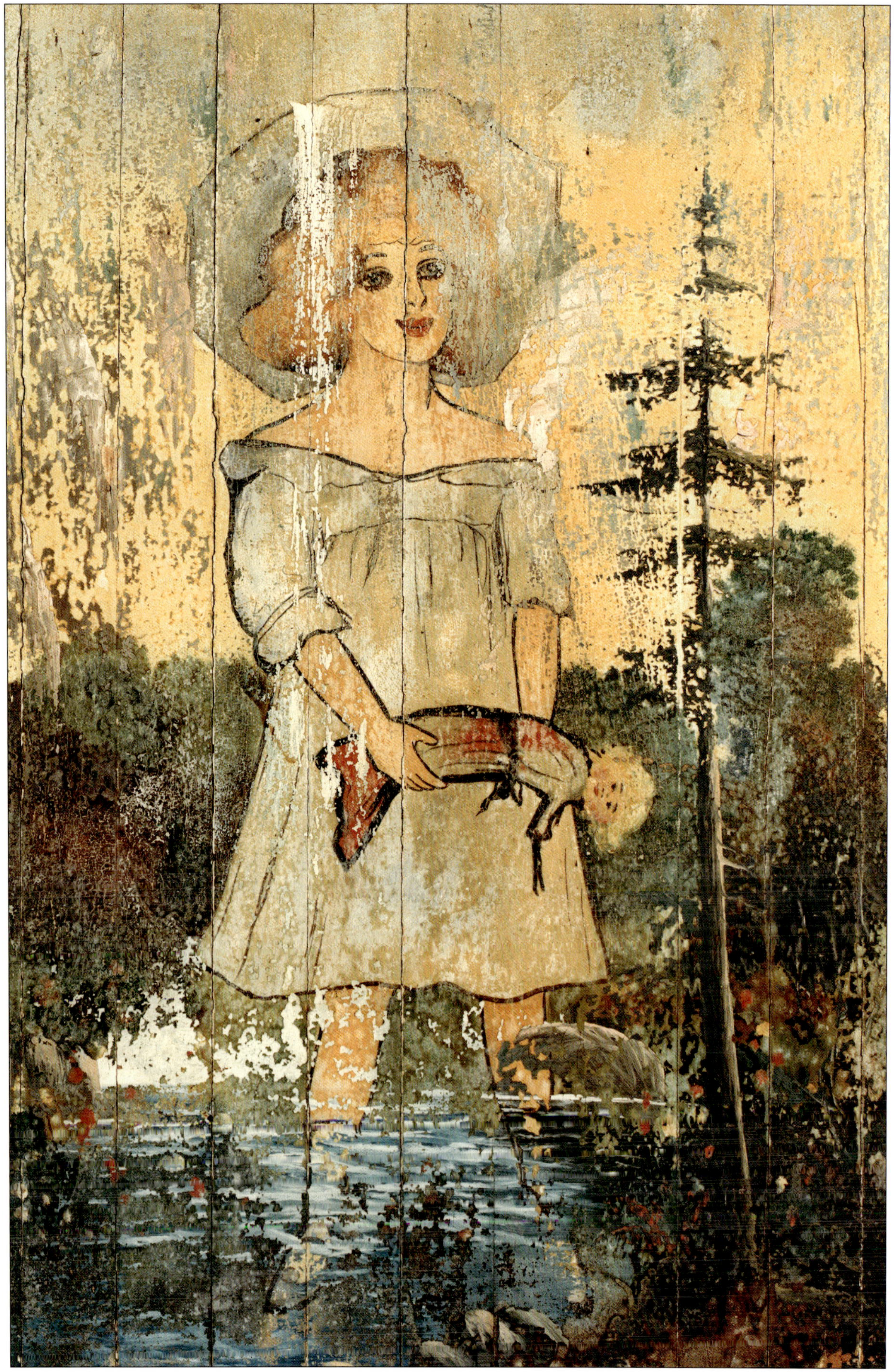

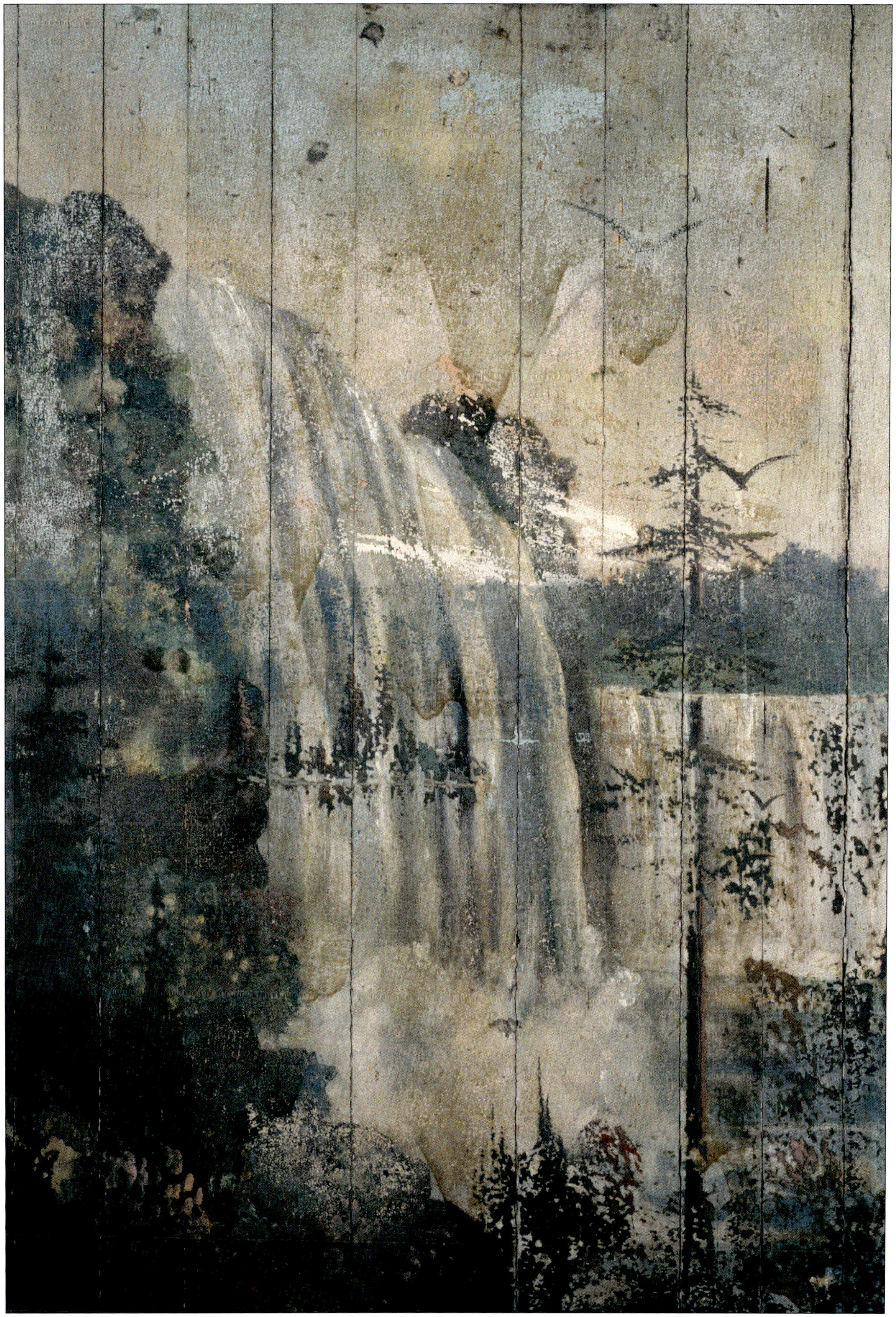

PANEL 12

PANEL 13

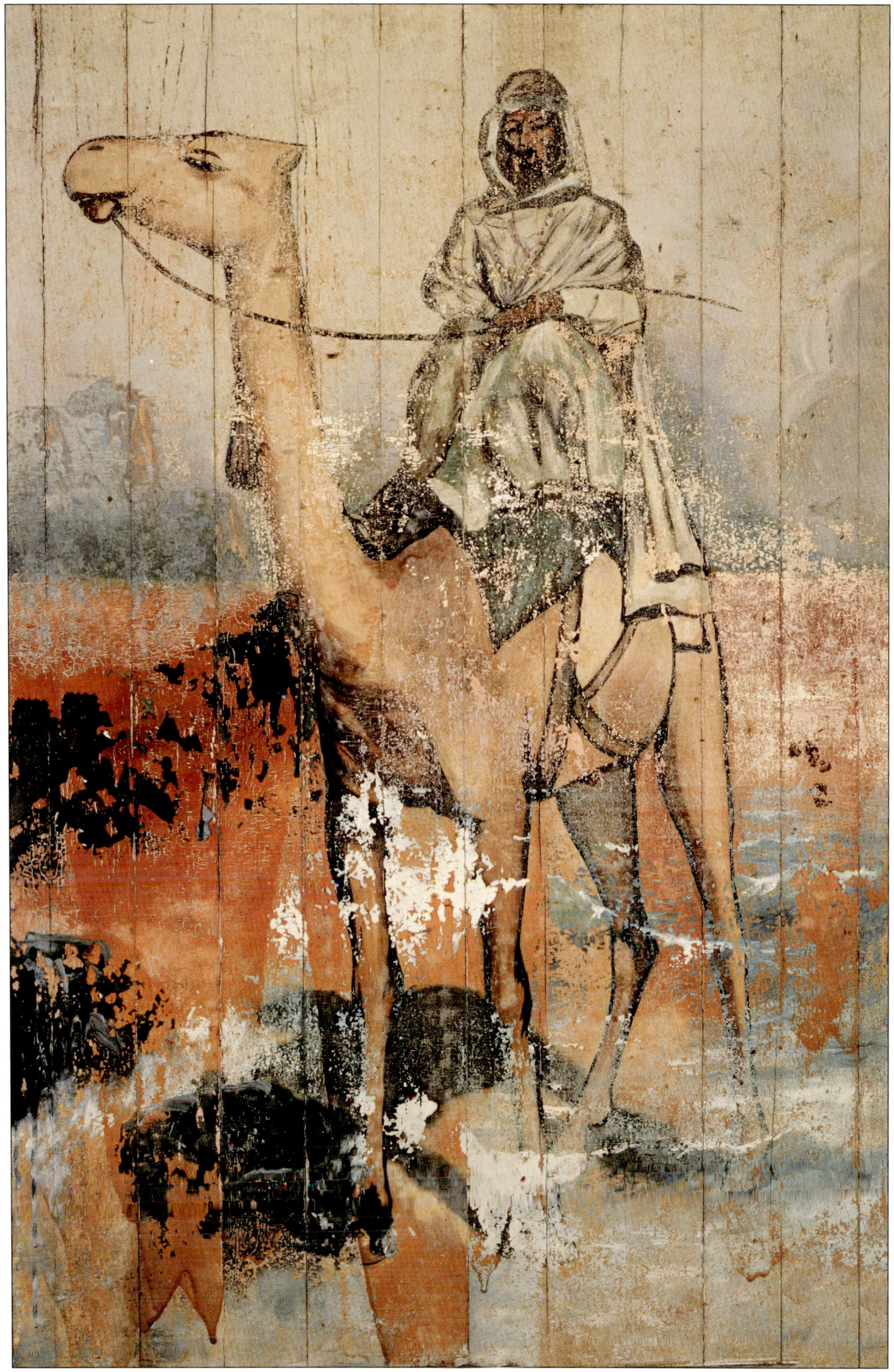

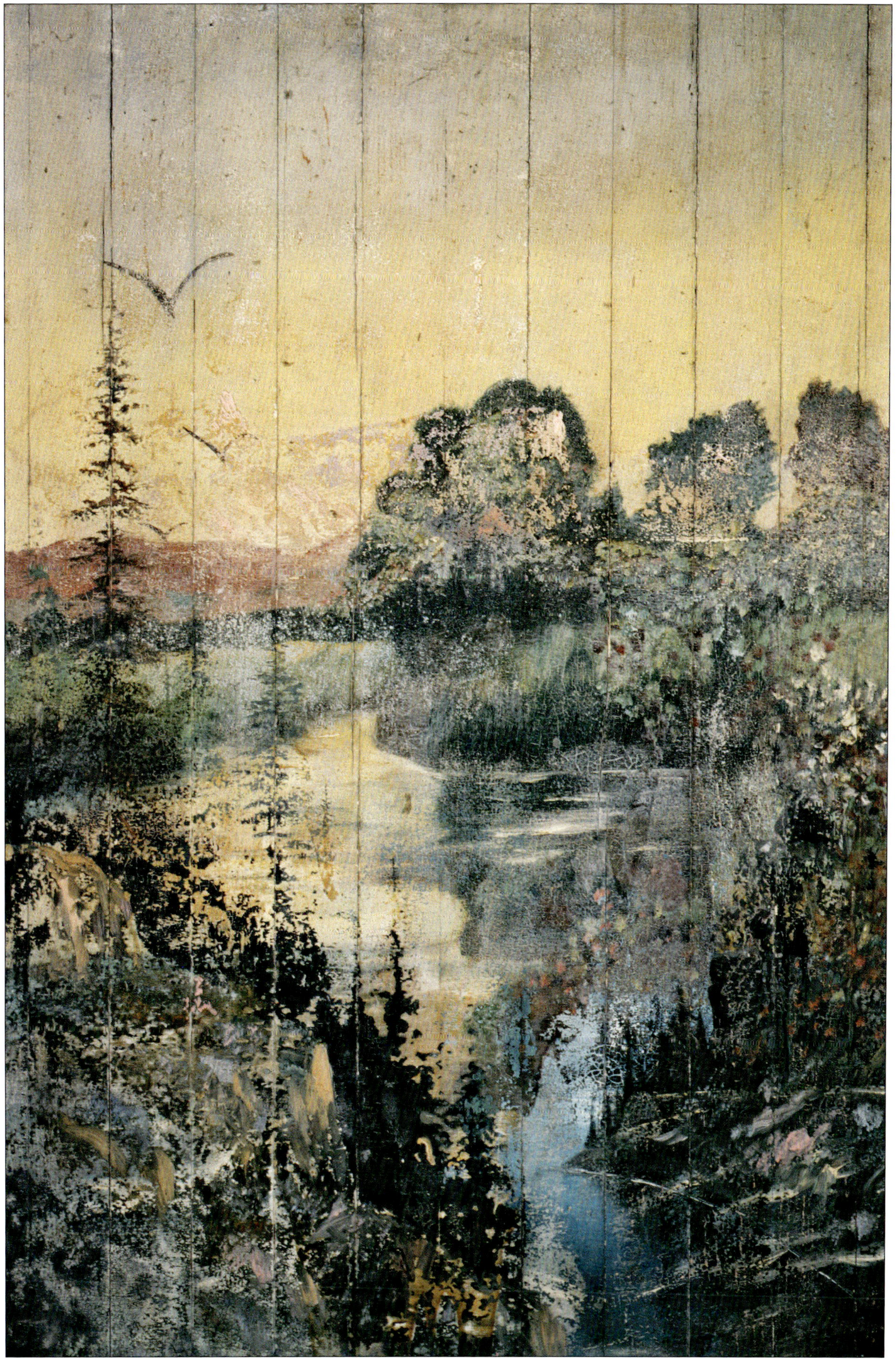

PANEL 14

PANEL 15

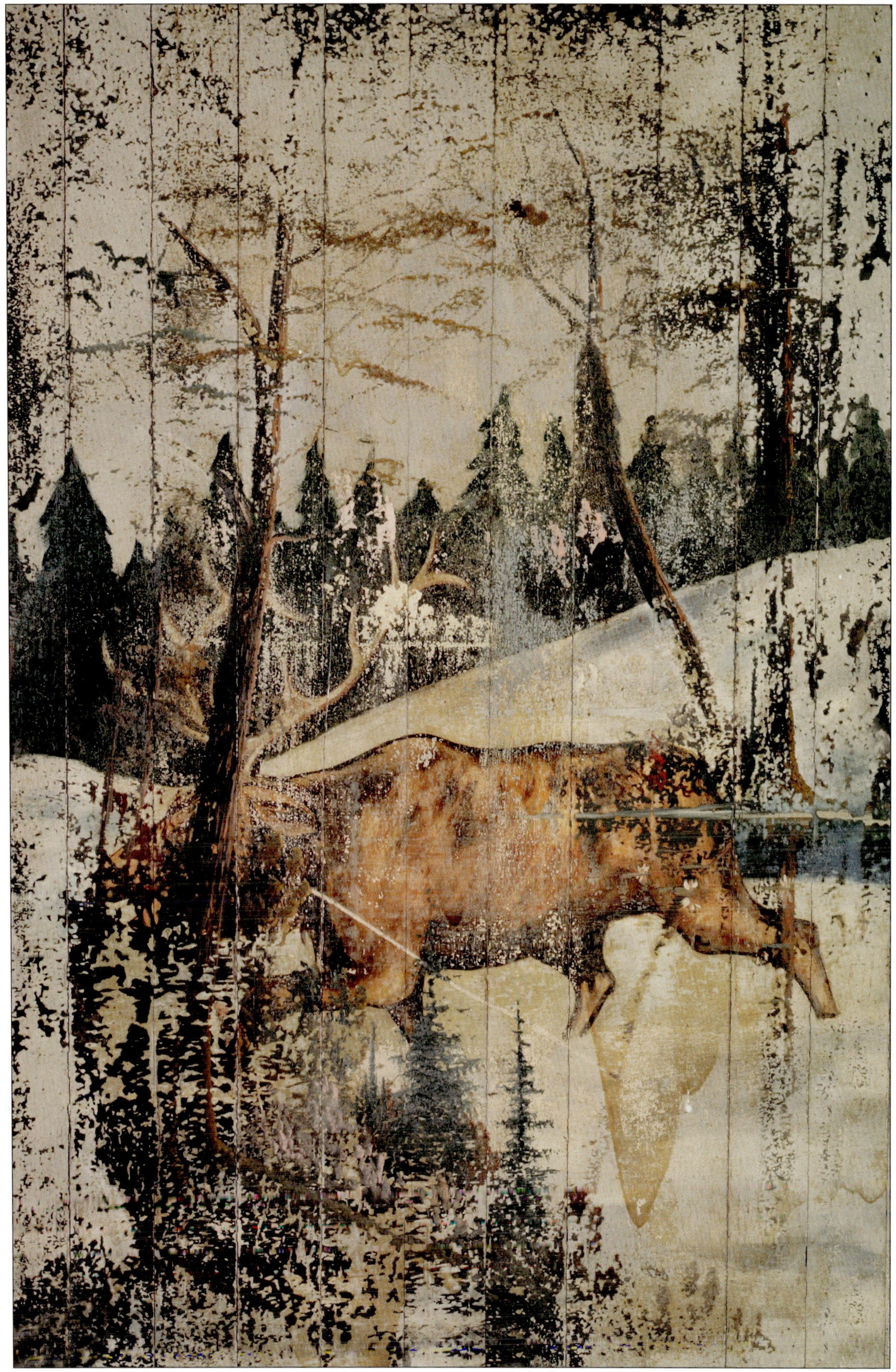

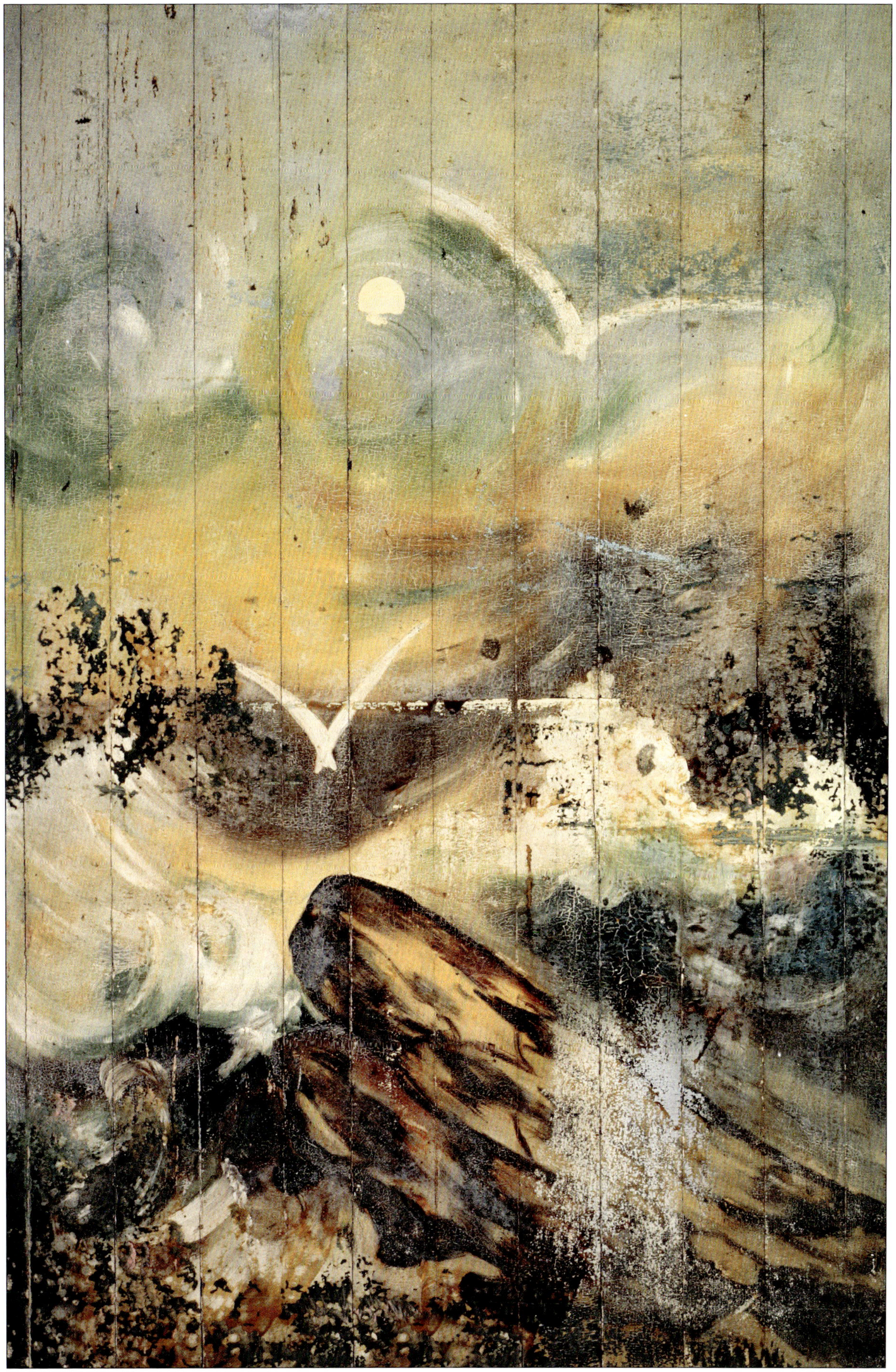

PANEL 16

PANEL 17

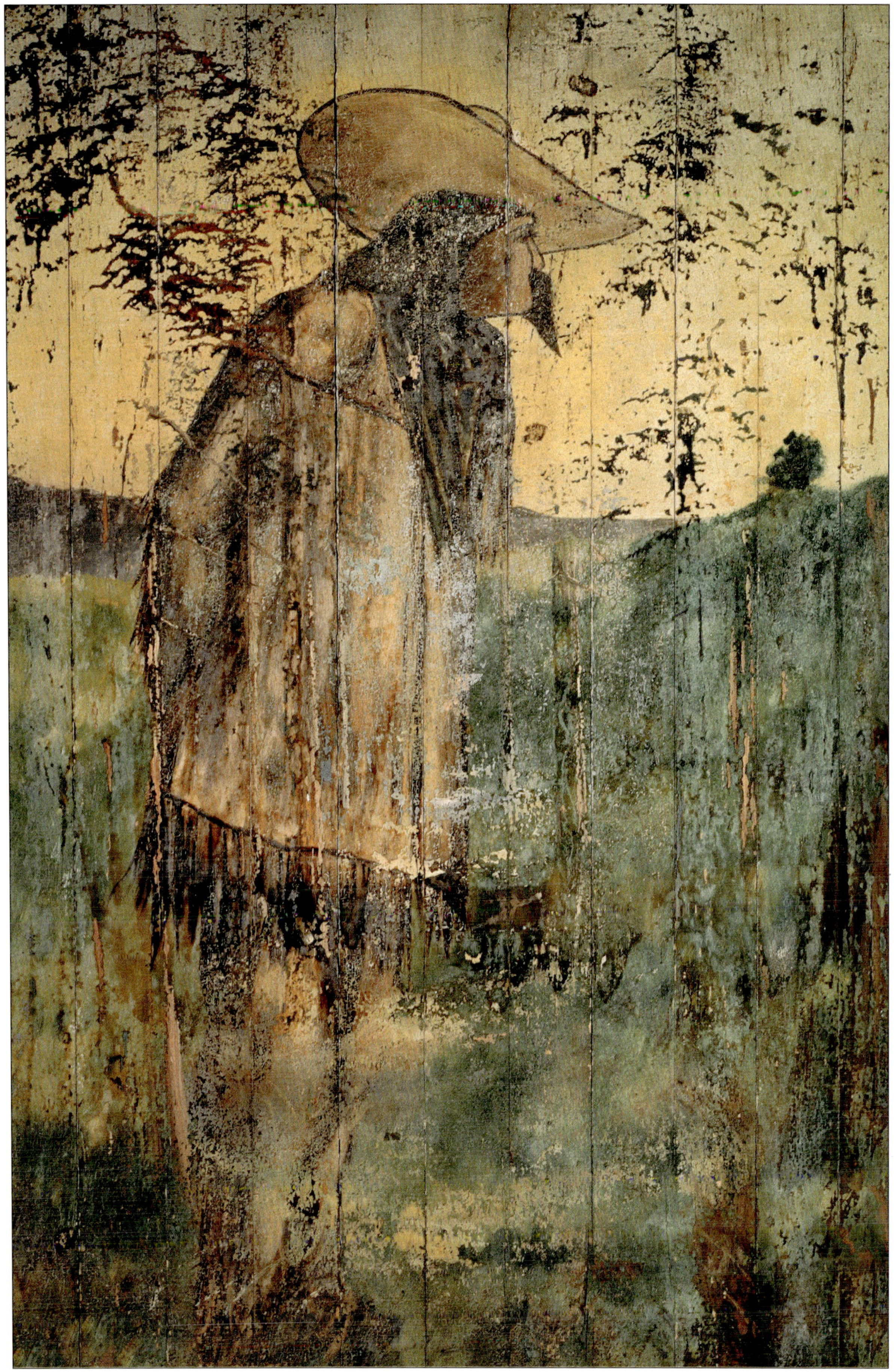

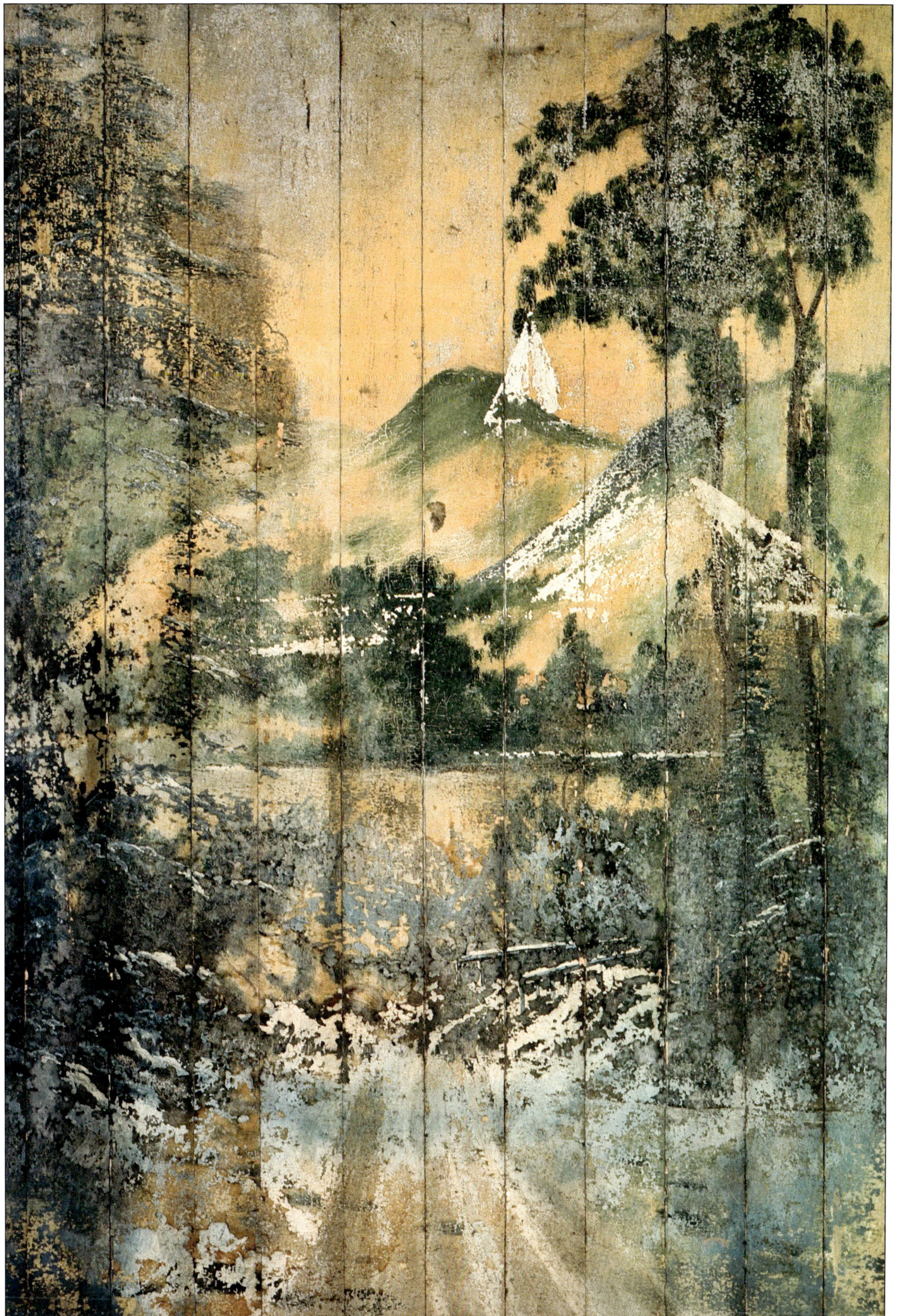

PANEL 18

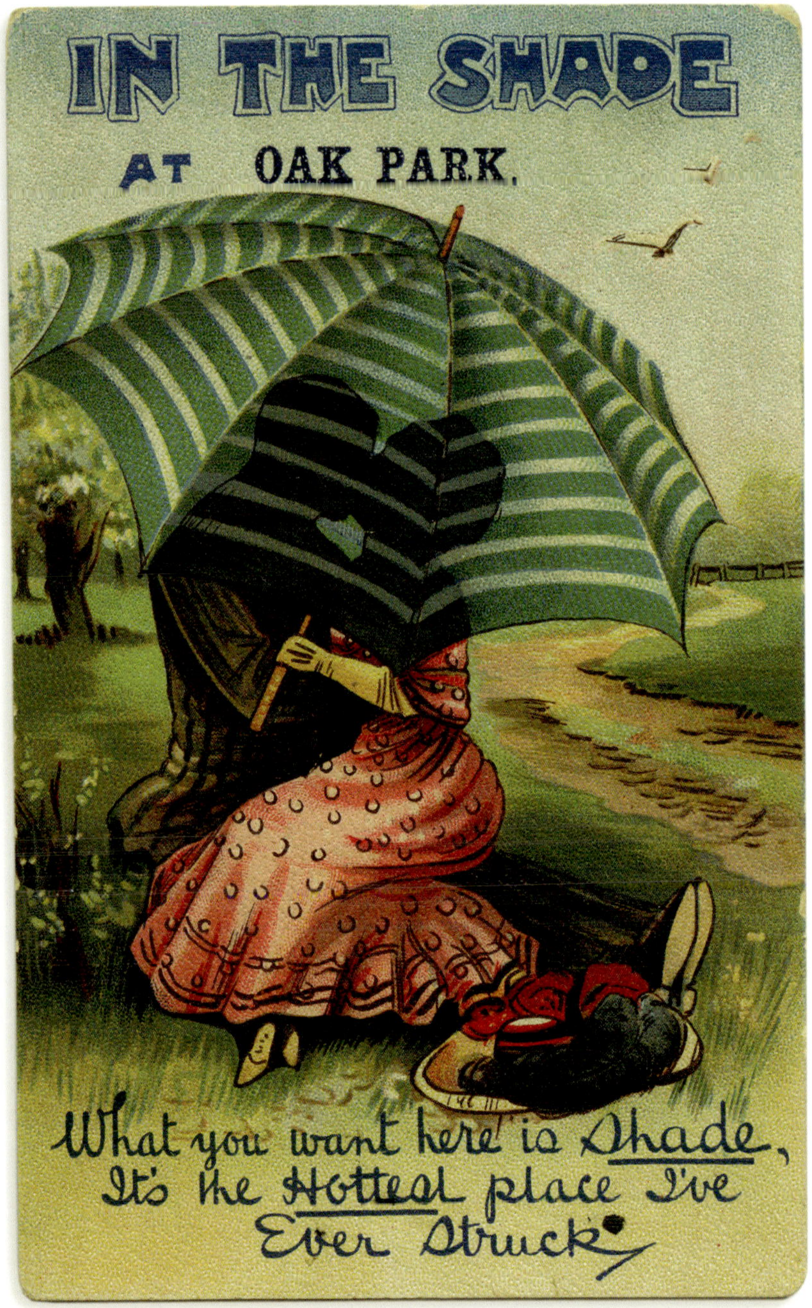
IN THE SHADE
AT OAK PARK.
What you want here is Shade,
It's the Hottest place I've
Ever Struck

AFTERWORD

by Prudence Roberts

THE ORIGINS of the "Noah's Ark" carousel that arrived at Oaks Amusement Park in 1923 became clouded over time by myths, often perpetuated through inaccurate newspaper reports and folklore. It was not built in Germany and floated upriver from the site of the 1905 Lewis and Clark Exposition; it was acquired from a floundering amusement park in Spokane, Washington, and had been built by the Herschell Spillman Company of North Tonawanda, New York, in 1912. But while its origins are not as colorful as the tales that have been spun around it, the carousel's life has in fact been more fascinating than the legends, and equally obscured by time.

The carousel originally featured a menagerie of colorful animals as well as eighteen painted panels encircling its center column. These paintings—the subject of our story—were, as we have learned, the work of anonymous German and Italian immigrant employees at the Herschell Spillman factory. The artists, whose names are long forgotten, were assigned specific images to repeat on the carousels they produced at a rate of about one a week. Mirroring the times, the sentimental paintings included an assortment of pastoral landscapes, idealized turn-of-the-century bathing beauties, an American Indian in full regalia, an Arab on a camel, and an explorer.

This exotic imagery disappeared from our carousel in the 1940s, when the panels needed attention. Rather than restore the now-dated Edwardian fantasies, Oaks Park management decided to bring local appeal to the carousel with scenes from the Northwest. We believe the resulting landscapes were the creation of the eccentric and talented brothers, Waldo Sporc Chase (1895–1988) and Wendell Corwin Chase (1897–1988).

The Chases, who were largely self-taught artists, spent their lives in Washington State, often living in teepees they designed and built themselves, exploring the wilderness and living simple and often impoverished lives devoted to nature and art. They studied a range of subjects, from botany to color theory, from writing and philosophy to Native American culture.

The brothers are best known for the prints they made early in their careers. In his memoir, *Teepee Fires*, Wendell cited the influence of a 1916 manual, Frank Morley Fletcher's *Woodblock Printing: A Description of the Crafts of Woodcutting and Colour Printing Based on the Japanese Practice*. The Chases used the term "Chenuis" (a Native American name for one of the peaks of Mount Rainer) as a trademark for the labor-intensive hand-tinted woodblock prints they made, often based on Wendell's photographs of landforms, lakes, and mountains. In their compositions and lyrical colors, these prints evoke the influence of not only Japanese prints and paintings but also the simple Arts and Crafts aesthetic so popular at the time.

In the 1930s, the Chases were active in the government–sponsored Public Works of Art Project (PWAP), one of the New Deal programs that brought employment to artists. At this time, their style changed somewhat, becoming more "Western," and they began

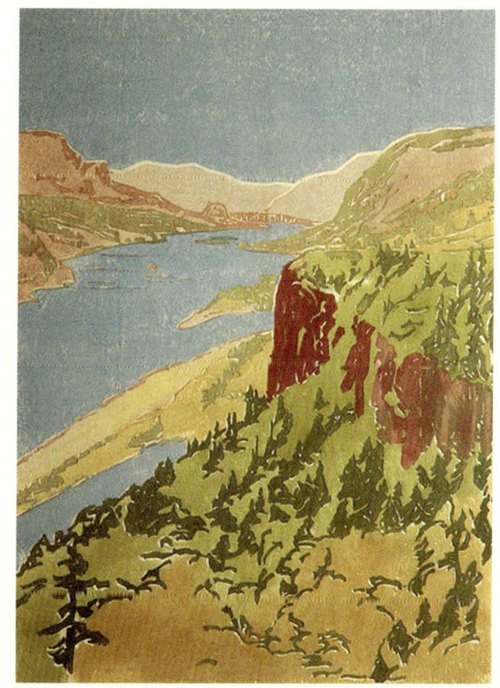

Columbia River Gorge. Woodblock print by Waldo Chase

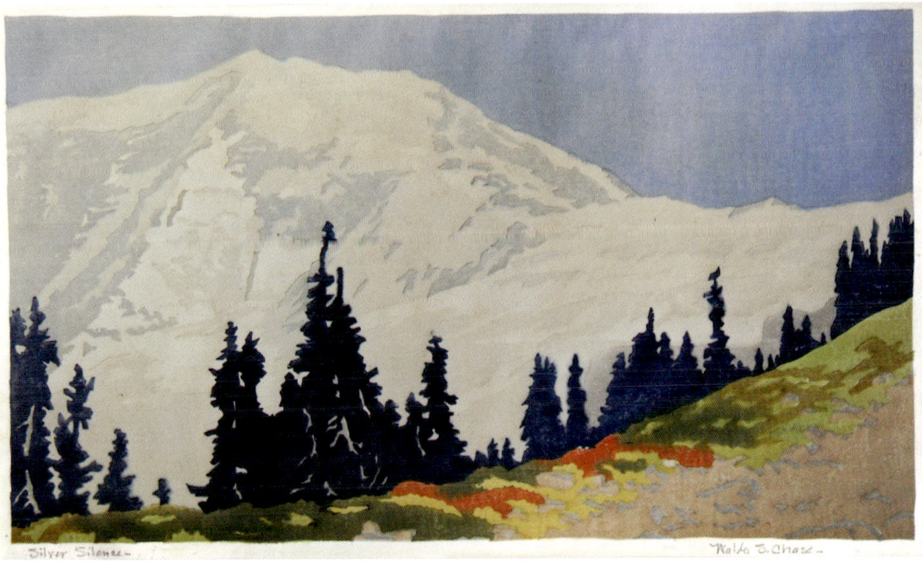

Silver Silence, Mount Rainier. Woodblock print by Waldo Chase

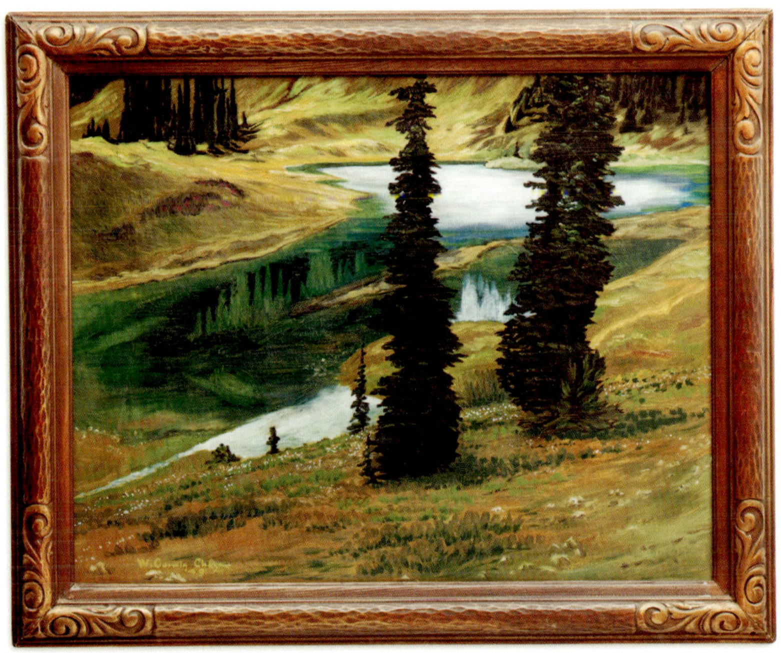

Lake Tipso. Painting by W. Corwin Chase, 1949

to put their energies into painting. When they were hired by Oaks Amusement Park in 1944, the brothers were established artists of the region—perhaps overqualified for the job they undertook. They spent about two months in Portland, devising the new compositions, some of which were based on postcards and snapshots supplied by Oaks Park employees. When the restored carousel made its debut in the spring of 1945, snowy mountains and forests, images of the Columbia Gorge Scenic Highway, the Oregon Coast, and the Vista House at Crown Point greeted the riders.

But the ravages of time, including two major floods (one in 1948, another in 1960), were not kind to the Chase brothers' work. Their evocative landscape paintings gradually eroded and flaked off, revealing fragments of the original paintings that lay underneath. The accidental, often surreal juxtapositions of figures and landforms created double exposures or *pentimento*, an Italian word for the underlayers that can become visible as a painting ages.

Such was the state of the panels when Jim Lommasson first saw them in 1970. In 1982, fearing that their current state was fragile, he set out to make a complete record of the images. The resulting photographs are the only visual record we now have of those first paintings, made by immigrant artisans, and of the Chase brothers' loving and evocative depictions of Oregon's landmarks. Because in 1985 the panels were "restored" yet again, this time by the Sam Jackson Crafty Art and Buffalo Grass Society. This latest incarnation incorporates subject matter and existing imagery from the past but lacks the subtle palette and aesthetic grace of its predecessors. Thanks to Lommasson, however, we have these photographs: a fascinating and beautiful testament to art found, and lost, and found again.

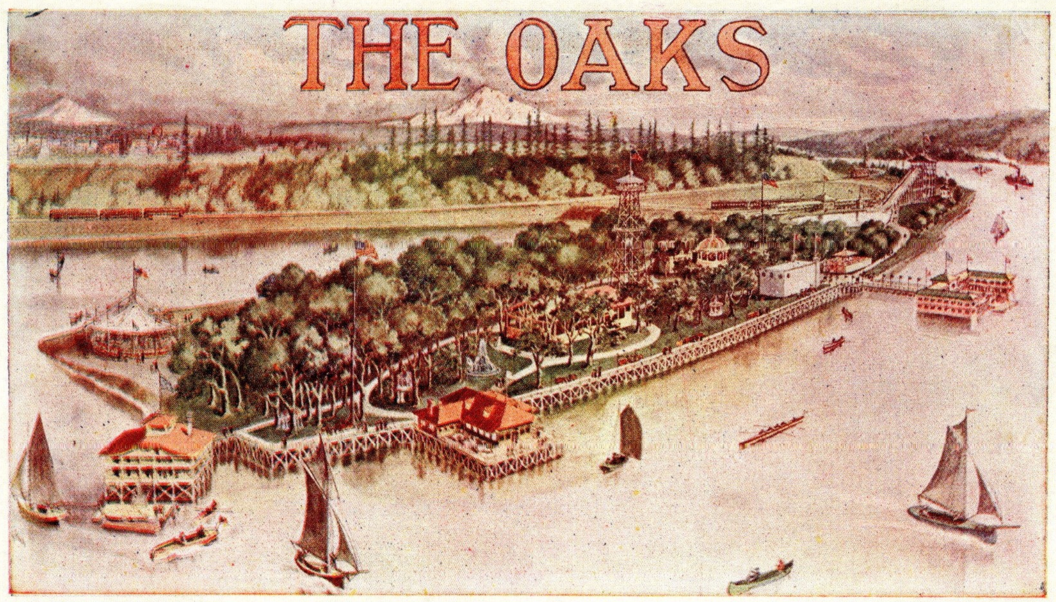

D. M. AVERILL & CO. PUBLISHERS, PORTLAND, ORE.

594 Portland's Coney Island on the Willamette River

ACKNOWLEDGMENTS

I would like to thank the following individuals and organizations for their assistance in the preparation of this book: Robert Bollinger ("Mr. Oaks Park"), Dana Beck, Tom Booth, Ruth Ann Brown, John Chilson, Mary Beth Coffey, Steve Connell, Steve Dotterrer, Katherine Dunn, Eileen Fitzsimons, Lawrence Fong, Jay Franklin, John Gattuso, David Gorsek, my teacher William Grand, Stewart Harvey, Therese Heynderickx, Harold Hutchinson, Kathy Ince, Rebekah Johnson, Steve Kenney, Bart King, Lawrence Kreisman and Glenn Mason (authors of *The Arts and Crafts Movement in the Pacific Northwest*), Cindy Lommasson, Lynette Miller at the Washington State Historical Society, Kate Mockler (curator of the Herschell Carrousel Factory Museum), Mark Moore, Erin Kirk New, Joe Norling, Oaks Park Association, *The Oregonian*, the Oregon Historical Society, Oregon State University Press, Chet Orloff, Michael Parsons, Sara Ellen Paulson, Portland Art Museum, the City of Portland Archives, Mary Ann Puls, Art Rich, Prudence Roberts, Tom Robinson, Jeff Roth, Angela Sanders, *The Sellwood Bee*, the Sellwood–Moreland Improvement League (SMILE), Tom Sheft, Katherine Spielmann, Brenda Stephens, Jennifer Stoots, Stewart Tilger, Terry Toedtemeier, Dody Tripp, Inara Verzemnieks, Thomas H. Wake, Mark Wexler, Robert Joki, Mom and Dad, and the woman with the parasol.

CREDITS

Page 1: The Oaks Ticket #106. Courtesy of Oaks Amusement Park — 2: 738 – *The Avenue Looking South, "The Oaks", Portland, Oregon.* Postcard. Courtesy of Mark Moore — 6: Oaks Park carousel as it appears today, showing the repainted versions of the original images, as executed by the Sam Jackson Crafty Art and Buffalo Grass Society. Photo by Jim Lommasson, taken in 2007. — 9: (top) Trolley arriving at the Oaks. Photographer unknown. Courtesy of Oaks Amusement Park; (below) The Laughing Gallery. Photographer unknown. Courtesy of the Sellwood-Moreland Improvement League (SMILE); (right) Oaks Amusement Park advertisement. Courtesy of Oaks Amusement Park — 10: (above) Oaks Park Carousel. Photographer unknown. Courtesy of Steve Kenney; (below) *The Jolly Gladway at the Oaks.* Postcard. Courtesy of Oaks Amusement Park — 11: Allan Herschell carving shop, circa 1922. Photo courtesy of Allan Herschell, from *Art of the Carousel* by Charlotte Dinger — 13: 5517. *On the Avenue at Oaks, Portland, Ore.* Postcard. Courtesy of Steve Kenney — 14: *"The Oaks" Portland Ore.* Photographer unknown. Courtesy of Bart King — 16: *Oaks Park Under Water #6, Portland, Oreg. 1948.* Photographer unknown. Courtesy of Steve Kenney — 17: *Landing at "The Oaks" on Willamette River, Portland, Ore.* Postcard. Courtesy of Mark Moore — 36: *In the Shade at Oaks Park.* Postcard. Courtesy of Steve Kenney — 37: *Columbia River Gorge.* Woodblock print by Waldo Chase. Courtesy of J. Franklin Fine Art, Inc., Seattle, WA — 38: (above) *Silver Silence, Mount Rainier.* Woodblock print by Waldo Chase. Courtesy of J. Franklin Fine Art, Inc., Seattle, WA; (below) *Lake Tipso.* Painting by W. Corwin Chase, 1949. Courtesy of Thomas H. Wake — 39: *The Oaks.* Postcard, Courtesy of Bart King. Every effort has been made to trace the ownership of copyrighted material and to make full acknowledgment of its use. If errors or omissions have occurred, they will be corrected in subsequent editions, provided that notification is submitted in writing to the publisher.